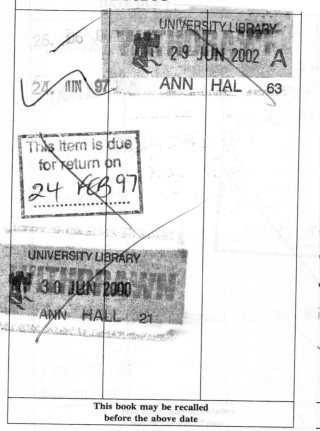

Studies in Sociology

Edited by

PROFESSOR W. M. WILLIAMS
University College, Swansea

9

THE SOCIOLOGY OF LEISURE

STUDIES IN SOCIOLOGY

THE
SOCIOLOGY
OF
LEISURE

Stanley Parker

London George Allen & Unwin Ltd
Ruskin House Museum Street

ISBN 0 04 301076 8 hardback   6000447547
     0 04 301075 X paperback

CC

Printed in Great Britain
in 10 point Times Roman by
Clarke, Doble & Brendon Ltd, Plymouth

ACKNOWLEDGEMENTS

The idea of writing a book on the sociology of leisure was originally that of my good friend and collaborator in several enterprises concerning leisure studies, Michael Smith. That his name does not appear as a contributor to this volume is due to other commitments which prevented him from taking a more active part and not to his lack of interest and encouragement. The structure and contents of Chapters 9 and 10 in particular, and of the book in general, owe much to discussions with, and helpful comments and suggestions made by Allan Patmore. Geoffrey Godbey, with whom I taught the sociology of leisure during a visit to the University of Waterloo, Ontario, enlarged my knowledge of the relevant North American literature and helped in many other ways. (In this book I have drawn on several chapters in G. Godbey and S. Parker, *Introduction to Leisure Studies and Services*, Philadelphia, Saunders, 1976.) Various other members of the Leisure Studies Group in Britain, and of what I like to look upon as the 'International Leisure Circuit' – I hope they will forgive my not mentioning them all by name – have contributed to the body of knowledge and ideas which is my subject-matter. There is not much that can really be called 'leisurely' about writing a book, but these various friends, colleagues and advisers helped to make lighter work of it. Finally I should like to thank Ena Challis for relieving me of the chore of final draft typing.

CONTENTS

Introduction

Until a few years ago the sociology of leisure in Britain (in so far as it existed at all) was treated either as a joke – comparable with the sociology of the bicycle – or as an adjunct of the study of work and industrial society. Today, not only has sociology itself become more widely accepted as a discipline, with its own teaching courses, expanding professional association and literature, but within it the study of leisure is also taking a greater part. There are many indications that this is a continuing trend.

A concern with the rightful place of leisure in sociological studies is not necessarily to support some of the more fanciful claims that a 'society of leisure' is already here or is about to arrive. I shall refer to these claims from time to time in the main text, and assess their validity in the concluding chapter. At the outset, it is perhaps desirable to recognise that leisure is only one of many factors in the long-term social development of mankind. It is not – at least for the majority of the world's population – an immediately pressing and vital issue. For some time to come the basic social problems of mankind will be with us: how to raise material living standards of the presently underprivileged to decent levels, how to develop industry without damaging effects on workpeople or the environment, how to formulate economic, political and social policies that will prevent destructive conflict, minimise unjustifiable inequality, and encourage a greater sense of individual participation in the life of the community.

However, just as there is more to individual life than work and other 'serious' preoccupations, so there is more to social structure than the conventional stamping-grounds of sociology such as industry, education, the family, and so on. It is time for the sociology of leisure to come into its own, not in a pendulum-like swing away from established sociological concerns, but in an attempt to relate leisure phenomena to those of the rest of life and of social structure.

Dimensions and relationships

If the sociology of leisure is part of the broad development of sociology as a whole, it follows that the theoretical approaches and methods of enquiry are not peculiar to leisure. One of the basic problems in any sub-field is to define its limits, and this is particularly important with a concept as slippery as 'leisure'. There are many ways of defining leisure, but most of them include one or both of the dimensions of time and activity. Leisure is time free from work and other obligations, and it also encompasses activities which are characterised by a feeling of (comparative) freedom. As with other aspects of life and social structure, leisure is an experience of the individual, an attribute of group or other social activity, and has relevant organisations and institutions which attempt to meet leisure needs, reconcile conflicting interests and implement social policies.

A narrow conception of sociology would imply a limited role for the study of leisure: the collection of statistics about time spent as leisure, admissions to sporting, entertainment or cultural events, the socio-economic and other characteristics of those engaging in particular leisure pursuits, and so on. A more comprehensive view is that the sociology of leisure properly includes such endeavours, but much more besides. Some of the key questions to which sociologists of leisure are attempting to find answers include: What is the relation of leisure behaviour to behaviour in other spheres of life? What are the similarities and differences between leisure and other institutions? How far does an understanding of leisure require an inter-disciplinary approach? Are there ways in which we can (and should) attempt to influence social policies which will affect the ways in which millions of people can have opportunities to enjoy their leisure?

The 'should' in the last question involves, of course, a value-preference, and some would argue that such statements are outside the purview of sociology. Thus Kenneth Roberts states flatly: 'The discipline of sociology is value-free; its principal job is to describe and explain how people in particular social situations use their leisure, and this contribution to our understanding of the significance of leisure can be made most effectively if the literature of sociology is kept as free from value judgements as is humanly possible.'[1] In expressing this preference for objectivity, Roberts is adopting a point of view with which many of us are in sympathy. Very few would want to see the field developed according to biased interests, research projects slanted to produce desired results, or controversial questions treated one-sidedly. But there is also something to be said for adopting a less detached attitude, exemplified by Alvin Gouldner: 'Unless the value references of sociological inquiry are made plainly evident, unless there are at least some bridges between it and larger human hopes and purposes, it must inevitably be scorned by laymen as pretentious word-mongering.'[2] Even if we can contemplate treating some aspects of social behaviour completely dispassionately, leisure is not an obvious candidate for such treatment. The fact that there is no consensus about what leisure is indicates that we need to recognise that we are dealing with a subject which is riddled with value-judgements and preferences.

Data and research

The undeveloped state of the sociology of leisure is reflected not only in the lack of theory-building and conceptual linkage with the main stream of sociological thought, but also in the paucity of research data. If one is content to define data solely in quantitative terms then some results have certainly been accumulated in recent years. Studies have been made of the leisure behaviour of particular groups of people, usually different age, occupational or locality groups. The personal and social characteristics of participants in specific forms of leisure activities – especially sport and outdoor recreation – have also received attention. Two national surveys of leisure, each involving several thousand interviews, have been published, although their coverage and lack of bias have been called in question.[3] From surveys of consumer expenditure it has been possible to form estimates of the proportion of total expenditure devoted to leisure goods and services in Britain.

Acceptance of all such data, however, begs the question of whether it is actually possible for 'leisure' to be measured. Critics can point to the fact that leisure has no standard method of measurement, and that attempts to measure it may really be measuring something else. With leisure conceived as experience of the individual, it is difficult to apply any standard definition for measurement purposes. Even with leisure conceived residually as free time, the problem is not overcome. The very idea of 'free time' is deceptively simplistic and, as Berger remarks, 'if sociology has taught us anything it has taught us that no time is free of normative constraint; what is work for some is leisure for others'.[4]

Just as in other branches of sociology, there is in the sociology of leisure a 'theory' part and an 'applied' part. Research is relevant to, and indeed is the life-blood of both parts. Research money is, of course, easier to obtain for 'practical' purposes than for contributing directly to the development of sociological theory, but it is to be hoped that the employment of social scientists on funded research projects adds idea-developing to head-counting. There is, however, the danger that 'applied' research, in being directed more or less exclusively to answering problems facing the sponsors, will neglect other and wider concerns, and lead to a distortion of the total picture. Thus we know much more about exposure to the media and about sport and outdoor recreation than we do about some of the more personal, informal and sometimes 'deviant' ways of spending leisure time.

A particular difficulty in relating empirical research into the use of leisure to theorising about the individual meaning and social significance of leisure is that most of the research evidence has been gathered during the last two decades. The lack of earlier data, except that filtered by a literate elite unrepresentative of the common people, makes it extremely difficult to place the contemporary phenomena of leisure in historical context. Much, however, can be done to draw together such data and interpretations as we have from societies in different parts of the world today, and this helps to place our understanding of specific leisure behaviour and institutions in wider perspective.

Inter-disciplinary emphasis

Although the main focus of this book is on the *sociology* of leisure, a full understanding of all the phenomena and significance of leisure requires the contribution of a number of disciplines and frames of reference other than those of sociology. The central concern of sociologists is with the interaction between individual behaviour and social structure: they study the relationship between leisure and its social context, including the social functions of leisure. Psychologists are more concerned with the dynamics of individual behaviour (and social psychologists with those of social behaviour): they pay particular attention to the functions that leisure performs for the individual. Despite the lack of historical data on leisure noted above, historians have much to contribute to our understanding of the role of leisure behaviour in earlier societies and hence of the variability of what has passed for, and acted as the equivalent of, leisure in societies different from our own. Similar remarks apply to social anthropologists, except that they have access to contemporary data while lacking (along with other social scientists) the time-span of the historian.

Social geographers have been prominent in recent writing and researching into leisure, and their special interest in spatial and environmental factors in the enjoyment of leisure is apparent and pertinent. Philosophy and religion have a stake in the study of leisure, if only because the qualities and values of 'the good life' involve some conception of how leisure fits into this. At a more mundane level, economists (at least those whose models allow for the playful as well as the rational element in man) can tell us about the demand for and supply of leisure goods and services, alternative leisure activities, and so on.

Apart from the social sciences and humanities, a number of academic disciplines and other professions can lay valid claim to an interest in leisure. Among those listed in the periodic *Directories of*

Leisure Scholars and Researchers[5] have been architects, biologists, botanists, journalists, market researchers, religious workers and teachers. These disciplines and professions are those represented by one or more individuals who happened to have responded to an invitation to be put in touch with other people studying and researching in some aspect of leisure: almost certainly they do not exhaust the list of disciplines that have a contribution to make to the study of leisure.

The sociology of leisure is involved in relationships of yet another kind: those between academics, whose prime interest is in data and theories, and practitioners of various kinds – planners, managers, administrators, etc. – who are concerned with practice and policies. It is, of course, possible to write a book on the sociology of leisure which is exclusively academic, or which is written from the standpoint that practitioners are welcome to make what they can of it with minimal assistance from the author. The present book aims to be helpful to non-academics without distorting the subject to cater to their particular needs. There is no need to sacrifice the standards of professional sociology for the sake of mass appeal or elite sponsorship, but neither is there virtue in living in an intellectual ivory tower.

The structure of the book

The book is divided into three parts which represent different approaches to the total subject area. In Part One we consider the context in which leisure, as we know it today, has developed. In so far as leisure existed in past and simpler societies in anything like the form we know it today, it was much more embedded in everyday life and had no separate institutions of its own. The coming of industrial society meant characteristic forms of non-work as well as work, out of which have grown the present institutions of leisure. For the different strata of society and for those at different stages of the life-cycle, leisure takes characteristic forms and carries various meanings.

Part Two consists of an examination of the relationship between leisure and other spheres of life. I have chosen to concentrate on four broad areas rather than to attempt to trace out every possible connection between spheres. The relation between leisure and work is so complex and intimate, and has in recent years been so relatively well researched and discussed, that it must have pride of place. Much leisure is spent in a family context, and the family has a formative influence on the leisure activities of its young members. Education *for* leisure and *as* leisure indicate the close relationship between these two spheres. A fourth chapter is devoted to the significant contribution of religious thinking to our understanding of the nature of leisure and of the overlap of religious and leisure behaviour.

In Part Three we turn to essentially practical concerns – areas in which sociology meets social administration, planning and the more social concerns of geographers, economists and suchlike. A thorough and detailed treatment of the matters dealt with in Chapters 9 and 10 would each require a largish book, though it is hoped that the main issues and problems are at least outlined in the present work. We consider first the various types of consumer demand for leisure and the factors which affect the level of demand. The other side of this coin is the arrangements which have to be made for public and private provision for leisure, including the important question of the aims of planning. Finally, we recapitulate some of the main points made in the book and discuss the question of whether we have or are developing a society of leisure, the trends in leisure which appear likely to continue, and the vital issue of the values which underlie leisure choices at both individual and societal levels.

REFERENCES

1   K. Roberts, *Leisure* (London, Longman, 1970), p. 9.
2   A. W. Gouldner, 'Anti-Minotaur: The Myth of a Value-Free Sociology', in M. Stein and A. Vidich, eds, *Sociology on Trial* (Englewood Cliffs, N.J., Prentice-Hall, 1963), p. 43.
3   J. Curran and J. Tunstall, 'Mass Media and Leisure', in M. A. Smith *et al.*, eds, *Leisure and Society in Britain* (London, Allen Lane, 1973).
4   B. M. Berger, 'The Sociology of Leisure', in E. O. Smigel, ed., *Work and Leisure* (New Haven, College and University Press, 1963), p. 29.
5   Edited by M. A. Smith and S. R. Parker and available from the Department of Sociological and Political Studies, University of Salford.

PART ONE THE CULTURAL CONTEXT OF LEISURE

Chapter 1

A Historical and Comparative View

When people speak and write about 'leisure' they often use the word to mean different things. Therefore we shall look first at various definitions of leisure and related concepts such as free time, play and recreation. In order to put our modern ideas and experiences of leisure into wider context, we shall then examine what leisure means (if anything) to people in simpler, non-industrial societies. Many of the contemporary propositions which are being put forward about what leisure is or should be are based on ideals which were first formulated in ancient Greece and which we review critically. Finally, we shall outline the historical changes in leisure since medieval times, paying particular attention to time available and the experience of leisure in relation to work.

Definitions and concepts

There are three broad ways of defining leisure.[1] One is to take the twenty-four hours in the day and subtract from them periods which are not leisure: working, sleeping, eating, attending to physiological needs, and so on. Clearly there is scope to disagree about what should be taken out of the twenty-four hours in order that only leisure should be left: for example, cannot eating in sociable and comfortable surroundings be experienced as leisure? Other possible things to take out of total time to leave only leisure include travelling to and preparing for work, meeting obligations toward others, and working around the home. This type of definition may be called 'residual', and a typical example is that given in *The Dictionary of Sociology*: leisure is 'time devoted to work, sleep, and other necessities, subtracted from twenty-four hours – which gives the surplus time'.[2]

A second type of definition of leisure insists that it is essentially not a period of time but a quality of activity or of the person engaging in the activity. Such definitions are favoured by religious and philosophical writers: thus the Catholic Josef Pieper conceives of leisure as 'a mental and spiritual attitude – it is not simply the result of external factors, it is not the inevitable result of spare time, a holiday, a week-end or a vacation. It is . . . an attitude of mind, a condition of the soul . . .'.[3] Similarly, a Protestant view of leisure identifies it with qualities of refinement, holding it to be unique because it is often associated with spiritual or artistic values.[4] (We shall deal more fully with the relation between leisure and religion in Chapter 8.) Also, some sociologists use this type of definition, often with an emphasis on the quality of freedom: thus Touraine conceives of leisure as freedom from rules and from accepted or socially imposed models of behaviour.[5] Unavoidably this type of definition involves value-judgements, that is, statements about what attributes of the activity or the person we think are desirable.

A third type of definition seeks in effect to combine the other two. To start with, there is a *residual*, or time definition, accompanied by a *normative* statement about what leisure ought to be. To take two examples from many possible ones: leisure is 'the time which an individual has free from work or other duties and which may be utilized for purposes of relaxation, diversion, social achievement, or personal development'.[6] Or it is 'a number of occupations in which the individual may indulge of his own free will – either to rest, to amuse himself, to add to his knowledge or improve his skills disinterestedly or increase his voluntary participation in the life of the community after discharging his professional, family and social duties'.[7]

An adequate understanding of leisure requires that we take into account both its time and activity dimensions. The amount of time we have for leisure determines what we can do in that period – whether we can only snatch a quick break from a heavily committed schedule or undertake a lengthy process of learning a new leisure skill like playing a musical instrument or travelling to a distant part of the world. On the other hand, it would be unwise to think that leisure is simply 'free time'. People who become unemployed or who retire on low incomes usually have plenty of 'time on their hands', but very likely they do not feel that they have true leisure (*enforced* leisure is really a contradiction). Gordon Dahl writes: 'the leisure that people need today is not free time but a free spirit; not more hobbies or amusements but a sense of grace and peace which will lift us beyond our busy schedules'.[8]

Once we have developed a general approach to leisure, and have some idea of how to distinguish what is and is not leisure, we can begin to sort out various possible classifications. In this introductory section we can only touch on a few of these, and shall concentrate on types of activity, functions and meanings of leisure.

One of America's foremost scholars of leisure, Max Kaplan, offers the important insight that anything or any specific activity can become a basis for leisure, some of the main elements of which are: an antithesis to 'work' as an economic function; a minimum of involuntary social-role obligations; a psychological perception of freedom; a range from inconsequence and insignificance to weightiness and importance, often characterised by play.[9]

In classifying leisure activities, Kaplan suggests that we can ask such questions as: Are people the main concern of the activity? (visiting a sick friend). How important are rules? (playing a game). And does the person go to the world for the experience or the world come to him? (participating rather than spectating).

It is possible to analyse the functions, or purposes, served by leisure, either to the individual himself or to the society of which he is part. The French sociologist Joffre Dumazedier believes that leisure serves three main functions to the individual: 'relaxation, diversion, or broadening his knowledge and his spontaneous social participation'.[10] Relaxation may be seen as recuperation from daily pressures, entertainment is the antidote to boredom, and the third function encourages the development of the personality. On the other hand, Edward Gross seeks to show that leisure has certain functions for the social group or for society itself: thus the importance of work colleagues with whom one can take a friendly glass, and of sport as a focus of group and even national identification.[11]

Research has been carried out into the different meanings that leisure can have for people. Robert Havighurst concluded from his studies that different age, sex and social class groups can derive similar values from their leisure, even though its content is different.[12] The principal meanings (defined as felt satisfactions or reasons for carrying on a particular leisure activity) were in order of frequency: just for the pleasure of doing it, a welcome change from work, brings contact with friends, gives new experience, makes the time pass, and gives a feeling of being creative. Among the differences found were that more women said 'creative' and more working-class people said 'makes the time pass'.

The concept of play is related to that of leisure. All play is a form of leisure, but the reverse is not the case. Play, according to Charles Brightbill, is the free, pleasurable, immediate, and *natural* expression of animals, particularly the young.[13] The historian Johan Huizinga has made a searching study of play in different cultures and concludes that it is an indispensable element in all human civilisations and that it has five characteristics: it is voluntary and free; as an interlude in our daily lives, it is marked by disinterestedness; it becomes traditional and can be repeated; it creates order, rules becoming important for the existence of the play-community; and such a community tends to become permanent as an 'in-group' after the game is over.[14]

'Recreation' is a term that is often used to mean something similar to leisure. Recreation always indicates *activity* of some kind and, like leisure and play, it takes no single form. In its literal sense of re-creation, it may be seen as one of the functions of leisure: that of renewing the self or preparation for work. It is this element in recreation that has most commended itself to those who disapprove of 'wasted' or 'dissipated' leisure, an attitude that is positively summed up in the phrase 'wholesome recreation'. But it is also this very value-laden element in recreation that has led critics to compare it unfavourably with leisure. Thus Thelma McCormack writes: 'Recreation is a system of social control, and like all systems of social control, it is to some degree manipulative, coercive and indoctrinating. Leisure is not.'[15]

Simpler societies

In most pre-literate societies the majority of people worked – and still work – so hard to sustain themselves and their families that their lives were almost devoid of leisure in the modern sense. Leisure for the majority consisted partly in mere rest from toil, and partly in participation in stereotyped activities mainly of a ceremonial nature. Participation in such rituals was not regarded as 'leisure' or 'spare time' by those who engaged in them but as part of the regular pattern of living.[16] The life of the peasant – and it must be remembered that the majority of mankind are still peasants – is a continuous round of labour. In the countries affected by the Hebrew tradition there is the Sabbath, but that is not so much a day of leisure as a day of ceremonial inactivity and of restraint.

To judge from this, however, that people in pre-literate societies had, and in pre-industrial societies today have, nothing equivalent to our leisure would be unwarranted. There is probably no *conscious* leisure, and hardly anything that is the result of the exercise of individual choice. In such societies most time is used, if not in work, then in other 'structured activities'.[17] Such festive occasions as weddings, christenings, birthdays and fiestas are common but, although they have an obligatory character, they also serve as leisure activities.

In simpler societies the line between labour and leisure is not sharply drawn. Primitive people tend to approach a great many of their daily activities as if they were play. The orientation of life is toward long periods of work interspersed with occasional periods of intense expenditure of energy. In these societies there are no clearly defined periods of leisure as such, but economic activities, like hunting or market-going, obviously have their recreational aspects, as do singing and telling stories at work.[18] Though there are things done for enjoyment and recreation, the idea of time being set aside for this purpose is unfamiliar.

Anthropologists who have studied the daily lives of people in simpler societies report a pattern of work and leisure that is much more integrated than most of ours in modern industrial society. Thus 'a striking feature of Maori culture is the way in which every aspect of their economic life was permeated with a definite element of recreation. Whether engaged in fishing, bird-snaring, cultivation of the fields, or building a house or canoe, the occasion was marked by activities which we could definitely classify as recreational.'[19] These activities – singing, loud talking, laughter – are also features of the co-operative work parties which are to be found in many parts of Africa. Hortense Powdermaker reports that in African tribal life men and women enjoyed leisure not according to 'clock time' but whenever they were free from the routine duties of daily life.[20] Tribal rituals on the occasion of birth, initiation, marriage and death were a significant part of religion, but the feasts, the dancing and the beer-drinking likewise provided a welcome break in the monotony of daily life. Economic, ritual, religious and leisure activities were not as sharply differentiated temporally or spatially as they are in modern society.

One of the biggest differences in the meaning of leisure is that between urban and rural communities. Leisure in agricultural societies is structured by the rhythm of necessary daily tasks and of the seasons, and is embedded in life rather than a separate part of it. The point is illustrated by the reaction of Texan homesteaders to the possibility of inheriting a large fortune. Some thought they would take time off to go hunting and fishing, but no one considered complete leisure a possible way of life.[21]

However, some pre-industrial societies do make a distinction between work and leisure that is quite close to our modern one. For example, the lives of the Baluchi of Western Pakistan are divided into a sphere of duty or obligation and an area which they call the sphere of one's own will.[22] The latter is their cherished area, the one in which they spend their energy and imagination and ingenuity. This pattern of life may be compared with one Chinese view that leisure time is like unoccupied space in a room. It is the unoccupied space which makes a room habitable, as it is our leisure hours which make life endurable.[23]

Greece and the leisure ideal

The idea that leisure is something more than mere free time dates back to the classic philosophers of ancient Greece, notably Aristotle and Plato. Many modern writers on leisure refer to and discuss Greek conceptions. These are important, both in understanding subsequent philosophies of leisure and in offering a possible way forward in a materialistic age when some observers believe we stand in need of a sense of direction in our society and in our own lives.

The Greek view of leisure was based on its association with 'schooling' or cultivation of the self, rather than with free time. The original meaning of the Greek word *schole* was to halt or cease, hence to have peace or quiet. Later it meant time to spare or, specially, time for oneself. But, as Sebastian DeGrazia warns us, this is not to say that the ancient Greeks saw leisure *simply* as free time: 'one senses a different element, an ethical note, a hint that spare time when misused is not leisure. . . . Leisure is a condition or a state – the state of being free from the necessity to labor.'[24]

The contrast of leisure was not just with work. There was also a contrast with action. Aristotle spoke of the life of leisure versus the life of action. But he went further to insist that no occupation can be leisure and that leisure cannot be anything related to an occupation. The goal of being occupied should, thought Aristotle, only be to attain leisure, or, as it may be more popularly translated, 'we are unleisurely in order to have leisure'. On this view, work and things which are necessary because of work could have nothing to do with leisure. Thus amusement and recreation could not be leisure, since they were regarded as necessary because of work. Rather, they were related by Aristotle to un-leisure and were identified as curatives for the stress and pain which were implicit in the lack of leisure.[25] Instead leisure was conceived as a state of being in which activity is performed for its own sake or as its own end.

The Greek conception of leisure was really part – though a very central part – of a wider conception of the nature of a free man. The Greeks saw the capacity to use leisure rightly as the basis of the free man's whole life. The actual range of activities which qualified as leisure was, however, severely restricted. Aristotle cited only two as worthy of the name leisure – music and contemplation. It is clear that the latter is the key to understanding the Greek ideal of leisure, since musical activities were valued for their contribution to the cultivation of the mind. Both Aristotle and Plato prized contempla-tion above all other activities. 'The man in contemplation is a free man. He needs nothing. Therefore nothing determines or distorts his thought. He does whatever he loves to do, and what he does is done for its own sake.'[26]

It would be wrong to suppose that such ideas as these were intended only as personal philosophies or to be debated only in cloistered isolation from the rest of civil society. DeGrazia explains the link with politics as follows. If a man is at leisure only when he is free, the good state must exist to give him leisure. What he does in this leisure can be equated with what we today call the good life. The life of leisure was the only life fit for a Greek.

There are, of course, many objections which can be raised to this whole conception of leisure. Prominent among these is the fact that Greek society was based on slave labour; the style of life and leisure regarded as appropriate to 'free men' was in fact that of a privileged elite. It may be that technological and social advances will make it possible in the society of the future for the mass of people to be free from the necessity to work and hence free to fill their lives with music and contemplation. But to rule out from leisure the whole range of creative activities beyond those two, and which people in post-Greek societies have chosen when free from economic necessity, would be unnecessarily to narrow the experience of leisure. It would also fail to achieve that wider cultivation of the mind which was central to the Greek ideal of leisure.

It is also relevant to point out that what we have been discussing is the Greek leisure *ideal*, which is not necessarily consistent with the Greek leisure *practice*. Attention to games constituted part of the education of the leisure, i.e. privileged, class.[27] Military needs led to a heavy emphasis on physical feats of daring, accuracy and endurance. The early Olympic Games included foot races, wrestling, boxing, chariot-racing and oratory. The large stadiums and gymnasiums housed athletic activities, whereas open-air amphitheatres afforded areas for music, dance and dramatic festivals. The Academy fostered intellectual and aesthetic activities, whereas the Forum, or public square, provided an opportunity for public discussion. The public baths offered a setting for diversion and relaxation. So perhaps it is fair to say that, for some of the people then and most of the people today, there was not so much difference between the range of leisure opportunities. On the other hand, the leisure ideal was for a minority then, and probably remains for a different minority today.

The history of leisure in Britain

Since this is a book on the sociology, rather than the history, of leisure, I shall not attempt a comprehensive review of the ways in which leisure has developed, declined and changed in Britain over the past few centuries. Instead I shall sketch a number of observations which may serve as a framework (or at least as a series of pointers) for a larger historical account yet to be undertaken. These observations chiefly concern changes in the amount of time available for leisure and the experience of leisure in relation to work.

In earlier times the number of days of leisure (free time) enjoyed by the ordinary working man were much greater than during the Industrial Revolution. About one day in three was a holiday of some kind. Estimates of annual and lifetime leisure suggest that the skilled urban worker has only recently regained the position of his thirteenth-century counterpart.[28] The trend in manual occupations was towards longer hours from the late Middle Ages to around 1800, and in the mid-nineteenth century the average working week for factory workers was seventy hours or more. Farm workers were exceptions to this trend: estimates suggest that they worked very long hours during the whole period, with some reduction only in the twentieth century.

The decline of leisure from the Middle Ages to the height of the Industrial Revolution is not, however, to be measured only by the increase in working hours. In pre-industrial society work was part and parcel of everyday life and leisure was not a separate section of the day.[29] Work was carried on in the fields within sight of home or within the home itself, along with the friendly conversations and the business of village life. It was only when work came to be done in a special place, at a special separate time and under special conditions that leisure came to be demanded as a right. More precisely, 'time off work' was demanded, since there was no question that the intimate pre-industrial relationship between leisure and life could be restored in the factory towns of the nineteenth century.

These remarks apply particularly to wage-workers in factories: the situation among craftsmen and artisans was rather different, and it seems that in some cases they were able to keep a comparatively free use of their time even in the mid-nineteenth century.[30] Those who worked at home could – and by all accounts did – spend much of the early part of the week in leisure and in drinking if they were paid on Friday. It was not until Wednesday that the pressures of work might reassert themselves. Similar behaviour is recorded in weaving, pottery and elsewhere, even where a rudimentary form of workshop or 'manufactory' existed.[31] These were, however, the fortunate minority among the working class, and then, as now, they were outnumbered by those tied to the regular hours of factory or office life.

It is possible to argue that leisure never existed for the mass of people as a separate part of life until it was won from their excessively long working hours. On that view, leisure could be regarded as the product of industrial society, and indeed it does seem that the reduction in working hours was accompanied by forms of leisure typical of the social structure and circumstances of the time. The invention of the annual summer holiday is a nineteenth-century achievement and factory owners acknowledged 'wakes weeks' as regularised weeks of holiday, which were in effect traded in exchange for regular attendance at work.[32] In contrast to medieval 'leisure', which had to be justified by some kind of public ritual or celebration, the new leisure of the working class was largely filled by various amusement industries. Drinking was commercialised by the opening of licensed premises where evenings could be spent, horse-racing became a popular mass entertainment, and professional football and boxing followed the same path.

Industrial society is a mass-production and consumption society and this is evident in the conditions as well as the content of leisure. A predominantly rural economy gave way to the rise of towns: urbanism, in the classic phrase of Louis Wirth, became a way of life.[33] Urban man is extremely collective in both work and play; he is also non-traditional. Just as some of the old handicrafts still remain, so some groups of workers continue to enjoy traditional forms of leisure. For example, in Britain and France miners have their pigeon racing and breeding.[34] But for most people, for most of the time, leisure is commercialised and enjoyed more on an individual basis than as part of community or family life.

It is interesting to trace the ways in which leisure values have related to work values. Any society depends upon certain material products and skills but also upon the mass of people having, or at least acquiescing in, the appropriate values. Factories and offices are useless without people who can be persuaded to work in them. The Protestant or industrial view of leisure was – and to the extent that it lives on, is – quite different from the Greek ideal. The Protestant ethic ennobled work and relegated leisure to the status of spare time, though spare-time activities could acquire value if used to restore men for work. But another force was operating within capitalism which was to have wide implications for the future of leisure. Economic expansion needed people willing and able to consume the products and services of industry. A new and lucrative market for these products and services was found in mass leisure. We shall deal more fully with this development in Chapter 2.

REFERENCES

1 A fuller discussion of definitions is in S. R. Parker, *The Future of Work and Leisure* (London, Paladin, 1972), pp. 20–5.
2 H. P. Fairchild, ed. (New York, Philosophical Library, 1944).
3 J. Pieper, *Leisure the Basis of Culture* (New York, Pantheon Books, 1952).
4 K. Vontobel, *Das Arbeitsethos des deutschen Protestantismus* (Bern, Francke, 1945), p. 83 (quoted in N. Anderson, *Work and Leisure* (London, Routledge, 1961), p. 33).
5 A. Touraine, *The Post-Industrial Society* (London, Wildwood House, 1974), p. 212.
6 N. P. Gist and S. F. Fava, *Urban Society* (New York, Crowell, 1964), p. 411.
7 J. Dumazedier, 'Current Problems of the Sociology of Leisure', *International Social Science Journal*, No. 4, 1960.
8 G. J. Dahl, *Time, Work and Leisure* (Christian Century Foundation, 1971), p. 187.
9 M. Kaplan, *Leisure in America* (New York, Wiley, 1960), pp. 21f.
10 J. Dumazedier, *Toward a Society of Leisure* (London, Collier-Macmillan, 1967), pp. 16–17.
11 E. Gross, 'A Functional Approach to Leisure Analysis', *Social Problems*, Summer 1961.
12 R. J. Havighurst, 'The Leisure Activities of the Middle Aged', *American Journal of Sociology*, September 1957.
13 C. K. Brightbill, *The Challenge of Leisure* (Englewood Cliffs, N.J., Prentice-Hall, 1960), p. 7.
14 J. Huizinga, *Homo Ludens* (London, Routledge, 1970).
15 T. McCormack, 'Politics and Leisure', *International Journal of Comparative Sociology*, September 1971.
16 P. Bromhead, 'The State and Leisure', *Political Quarterly*, March 1964.
17 B. R. Salz, 'The Human Element in Industrialization', *Economic Development and Cultural Change*, October 1955.
18 K. Thomas, 'Work and Leisure in Pre-Industrial Society', *Past and Present*, December 1964.
19 F. Stumpf and F. W. Cozens, 'Some Aspects of the Role of Games, Sports and Recreational Activities in the Culture of Modern Primitive Peoples', *Research Quarterly of A.A.H.P.E.R.*, October 1947.
20 H. Powdermaker, *Copper Town: Changing Africa* (New York, Harper, 1962), p. 225.
21 E. Z. Vogt, *Modern Homesteaders* (Cambridge, Mass., Harvard University Press, 1955), p. 114.
22 R. H. Wax, 'Free Time in Other Cultures', in W. Donahue *et al.*, eds, *Free Time: Challenge to Later Maturity* (Ann Arbor, University of Michigan Press, 1958), p. 4.
23 Z. Nakhooda, *Leisure and Recreation in Society* (Allahabad, India, Katab Mahal, 1961), p. 4.
24 S. DeGrazia, *Of Time, Work and Leisure* (New York, Twentieth Century Fund, 1962), pp. 13–14.
25 P. C. McIntosh, *Sport in Society* (London, Watts, 1963), p. 23.
26 *Ibid.*, p. 21.

27 R. Carlson *et al.*, *Recreation in American Life* (Belmont, Wadsworth, 1972), p. 24.
28 H. L. Wilensky, 'The Uneven Distribution of Leisure', *Social Problems*, Summer 1961.
29 T. Burns, 'Leisure in Industrial Society', in M. A. Smith *et al.*, eds, *Leisure and Society in Britain* (London, Allen Lane, 1973), p. 43.
30 A. Clayre, *Work and Play* (London, Weidenfeld & Nicolson, 1974), p. 95.
31 E. P. Thompson, 'Time, Work-Discipline and Industrial Capitalism', *Past and Present*, No. 38, 1967.
32 J. Myerscough, 'The Recent History of the Use of Leisure Time', in I. Appleton, ed., *Leisure Research and Policy* (Edinburgh, Scottish Academic Press, 1974).
33 L. Wirth, 'Urbanism as a Way of Life', *American Journal of Sociology*, July 1938.
34 J. Mott, 'Miners, Weavers and Pigeon Racing', in M. A. Smith *et al.*, eds, *op. cit.*

Chapter 2

Leisure in Industrial Society

Leisure is, among other things, a social institution, and in this chapter we shall be concerned with its forms and structures in modern industrial societies. Social stratification is an important ingredient in modern societies, and the leisure of individuals is influenced by their class or status position, though some would argue that this influence is now less than in the past. The growth of the commercial leisure industries has helped to shape the way in which most people enjoy much of their leisure. A notable feature of industrial societies is that 'food famine' has given way to 'time famine', with special implications for leisure behaviour. We shall briefly review some of the variations in leisure behaviour between industrial societies, though the similarities appear more marked than the differences.

Leisure as a social institution

The claim that leisure is essentially a product of modern industrial society has been put forward by several writers and researchers in recent years. The thought is expressed in different ways, and emphasis is laid on different consequences of the process, but the similarity of the basic propositions is not hard to detect. Tom Burns argues eloquently that 'social life outside the work situation has not re-emerged; it has been created afresh, in forms which are themselves the features of industrialism, which derive from it *and which contribute to its development, growth and further articulation . . .*'.[1] Joffre Dumazedier claims that the two preliminary conditions which make it possible for the majority of workers to gain leisure (the diminution of ritual obligations prescribed by the community and the demarcation of remunerated work from other activities) exist only in industrial and post-industrial societies.[2] In a more conventional sociological vein, Kenneth Roberts states that 'since the industrial revolution a general process of structural differentiation within society has taken place with special institutions emerging to cater for needs such as education and social welfare which were previously catered for by multi-purpose groups and organizations. Leisure is just one amongst man's social activities which has been subjected to a process of structural differentiation. . . .'[3]

Putting together the propositions of these three writers, leisure in industrial society may be seen as the concomitant – essentially the *reaction* to – work in industrial society, as the consequence of increased individual freedom, and as emerging with its own characteristic social institutions. But there is more to this already complicated process than that. In being a reaction to work, 'industrial leisure' is at the same time something more: it is an alternative source of ethical values to those founded in production and work (this has implications for the class structure of society, which we shall consider below). In being a beneficiary of the greater productivity made possible by mass production and marketing, leisure tends to exhibit the same features and social relationships which mark the world of industrial work: standardisation, routinisation, a drive to capital intensity rather than labour intensity, the outnumbering of participants and those active in controlling their work and leisure lives by spectators and those subservient to some mechanical or social process. Finally, the emergence of characteristic leisure institutions means that such institutions are important determinants of the way in which people spend their leisure – the institutions do not merely meet a demand, but play a major role in creating it and in deciding *how* it shall be met.

In some ways the 'institutional' approach to the analysis of leisure represents an alternative to the 'cultural' approach to be discussed in the following chapter. This is even more apparent if we contrast 'cultural' with 'structural'. If leisure is indeed a product of industrial society, then we should expect societal influences to be stronger than individual ones, and the similarities between the ways in which people spend their leisure to be greater than the differences. There is no simple way to make such an assessment – indeed, one of the major tasks of the sociology of leisure may be seen as the study of the extent to which leisure *in* industrial society is the product *of* industrial society.

An important characteristic of any form of society is the type of relationship between the individual and collective representations of society such as the state or the government. If the key *economic* relationship in industrial society is that between capital and labour, the key *political* relationship is that between the individual and the polity (the institutions and relationships of society concerned with power). Leisure, as both individual behaviour and social institution, features in these relationships. In pre-industrial society, the pressures to conform with custom and practice were pervasive and direct – 'leisure' was a set of socially structured occasions and rituals. Industrial society brought more individual freedom – the pressures to conform became less direct, though arguably more pervasive.

It is tempting to define leisure in such a way that it fits the style and characteristics of industrial society and does not fit those of other types of society. Thelma McCormack seems to do this: 'I would suggest that leisure is dependent upon the extent of privacy and freedom from dissent. What encroaches upon and destroys leisure is repression, intolerance, a fixation on conformity. . . .'[4] Defined in this way, leisure becomes the product not only of industrial society but more narrowly of one particular form of industrial society: that which exhibits privacy, freedom from dissent, and so on. Dumazedier is guilty of the same cultural relativism: he argues that 'It would seem to us that from a sociological point of view there is no sense in making a comparison between the free time of the industrial society and the holidays, days off, etc., of the traditional societies. Time which has become free time because of economic development cannot be compared to the "empty" time of an "underdeveloped" economy.'[5] The answer to this is that there would appear to be a considerable sociological value in comparing and contrasting the socially structured non-work obligations of people in underdeveloped economies with the more individual choices open to those in industrial or post-industrial societies.

Leisure and social stratification in Britain

Just as opinions differ about the extent to which contemporary Britain is a class-divided society in terms of income and ownership, so they differ in respect of propositions about the differential effect of class position on leisure. Roberts believes that 'As far as the distribution of leisure time is concerned, Britain can be aptly called a democratic society. . . . It is no longer the case that a wealthy, predatory leisure class lives off the fruits of the labour of a class of work-ridden producers.'[6] There are two different propositions here: that leisure *time* is fairly equally distributed and that society is no longer divided into a leisure class and a non-leisure class. Let us examine these propositions separately.

One way of measuring leisure time is to assume that it is the residue after time at work is deducted. (This does not take into account time which is spent neither as work nor as leisure, but it may be further, if even more doubtfully, assumed that such time is roughly the same for all categories of people.) Official figures show that normal hours worked, i.e. excluding overtime, averaged in 1975 from about 36 per week in mining and quarrying to about 42 per week in agriculture, forestry and fishing.[7] Other figures suggest that the working week of British managers has averaged in recent years around 42–44 hours.[8] All these figures are, of course, for employees working full-time, and they lend support to the view that differences between occupational groups in time *available* for leisure are probably narrow. A better guide to time *devoted* to leisure is obtained from enquiries which specifically ask about this. Using a time-budget diary method, Young and Willmott give figures of 32 weekly hours of leisure for men, 26 for women working full-time, and 44 for women not in paid work.[9] Unfortunately these figures are not broken down by occupation or social class. My own survey of business, service and manual workers suggests that there *are* variations between such groups in the amount of subjectively-defined leisure time but that these differences are more due to type and degree of involvement in work than to economic or class position.[10] We may, in short, say that the available evidence supports the claim that leisure time is fairly equally distributed among employees in Britain, though this says nothing about non-employed minority groups such as the unemployed, the elderly, the chronically sick and those with enough capital to live without gainful employment.

The second proposition concerning leisure and social stratification is that people in different social strata (class or economic positions) enjoy roughly the same kind of leisure opportunities and experiences. This proposition is much less defensible than the first. It is true that, compared with earlier times, more leisure opportunities are available to ordinary working people: for example, it is probably only a slight exaggeration to say that the countryside 'has changed from being the area of escape for the privileged few to being the playground of the many'.[11] The rise of the mass leisure industries amounts, almost by definition, to a widening of the range of leisure goods and services which may be afforded by large numbers of people. But this is not to say that we have social equality in leisure. Leaving aside the loaded language of a 'predatory leisure class' and 'work-ridden producers', the extremes are nevertheless remarkable. For the rich there is pheasant shooting in Norfolk at £225 a day and grouse shooting in Scotland at £800 a week (1972 prices).[12] In the same year a grande-luxe suite on the liner *France* for a three-month world cruise cost £43,500. At the other end of the scale, were a massive 41 per cent of people in Britain who expected either to have no holiday that year or to stay at home.[13]

Britain, then, is a country in which time available for leisure is reasonably equally distributed (apart from the elite exceptions noted above), while opportunities for enjoying leisure retain in large measure a class-divided character. It is worth noting that in this respect Britain is not alone among industrial societies. In the United States there may be said to exist a class struggle of sorts over scarce free-time resources; for example some municipalities have passed legislation making it impossible for outsiders (who are more likely to be less affluent and possibly members of a minority group) to gain access to beaches.[14] To the extent that occupation determines class position, the inequalities in leisure are those of various occupational groups, which we shall consider in more detail in Chapter 5. But, involved in stratification, there are also cultural and educational elements which, while they may unite for leisure purposes individuals with the same cultural or educational experiences, serve also to divide those who do not share these experiences. There are, to put this point another way, not merely working-class leisure patterns and middle-class or upper-class leisure patterns, but also different class-based *approaches* to leisure in relation to other spheres of life and especially to work. Because of the values implicit in the concept of both 'class' and 'leisure', these differences are usually described in such a way as either to applaud or deplore them. They are applauded by W. H. Auden, who seems to regard as inevitable the restricted nature, but important function, of leisure in the lives of working people: 'among the many blessings enjoyed by a worker, not the least is the knowledge that for him leisure can never become a problem. He does not want and does not allow himself more leisure than he can cope with. . . . A labourer must find his happiness outside the activity by which he earns his living, and the most obvious place to look for it is in the field of personal relationships, particularly sexual relationships.'[15] Another view is that of those who regard only the intimate relationship between work and leisure, and not the existence of 'work-and-leisure classes', as inevitable. Such a view is expressed by Harold Entwistle: 'it may be that to solve the problems of dehumanising and trivial work will be to go a long way towards raising the quality of men's leisure preoccupations. In any event, there is a want of realism about those conceptions of education for leisure which assume that you can educate a man whose work is trivial and repetitive out of the pursuit of trivial, mechanical leisure activities.'[16]

The leisure industries

Industry, it has been remarked, needs the consuming time of workers as much as it needs their producing time.[17] Indeed, without a reduction in the long hours of work, and some rise in the purchasing power of workers enabling them to buy goods and services other than necessities, it is arguable that industry could not have developed, since no market for its products would have been created. With the reduction in working hours after the middle of the nineteenth century, the new leisure of the working class represented a vacuum which was largely filled by amusement industries.[18] During the last quarter of the nineteenth century the profits of the brewing trade were invested in building licensed premises where evenings could be spent, racing became a popular mass entertainment by the 1880s, and professional football and boxing followed the same path.

In Chapter 10 we shall examine the ways in which public and private enterprises cater for the leisure needs of people today. In the present preliminary review of leisure in industrial society, we may make some more general observations about the social forces which gave rise to and sustain the leisure industries. It should be noted that the pursuits catered for have been organised for a commercial market, or at least for a user public and, by and large, have been limited to what can be so organised. As Tom Burns points out, the development of the leisure industries has important implications for our interpretation of what has happened to relations between the social classes. Individual consumption had to be expanded to become the prime mover of economic expansion; the mass propensity to consume was in the interests of the industrial entrepreneur; and new ways of organising the spending of disposable income and time 'led to the evolution of new stratification systems and the blunting of the structural definition of classes through conflict'.[19]

This last statement is, of course, a particularly controversial one. It is not self-evident that raising the level of consumption of (leisure) goods and services leads either to a change in the stratification system or to a diminution in class conflict. Not all workers are 'affluent workers', nor does greater consumption of the output of the leisure industries necessarily lead to a rejection of class and class conflict.

Entrepreneurs in the leisure business are in some ways in a favourable, and in other ways an unfavourable, position. On the one hand, the leisure market is open ended. There is a limit to the amount a person can eat or drink, and a high income makes no difference to this limit. But there seems to be no limit to how much people who have money are prepared to spend it for pleasure – the market is 'elastic'. On the other hand, there is so much opportunity for individual choice that demand for a particular leisure product or service, influenced by the media, may rise or fall rapidly. This means that one leisure entrepreneur's profits may be at the expense of another's losses where both are in the same or competing sectors of the leisure industry.

Despite claims about growing permissiveness, there is still social control of much leisure behaviour through restrictions imposed on producers, distributors and consumers. Control of sources of commercial entertainment and pleasure is exercised through legislation, regulation and supervision. The licensing laws prescribe the hours of drinking in pubs, the number of greyhound meetings per track is restricted to two a week, commercial television operates under a franchise-granting authority, and so on. State and local-authority censorship of films for public showing continues, despite periodic attempts to abolish it.

Various associations have sought to achieve or maintain what they regard as desirable standards in leisure behaviour. They have, for example, concerned themselves with keeping Sunday free from leisure activities, getting certain books and plays banned, and keeping children off the stage. Also, there has been much local government opposition to the extension of bingo and betting-shop facilities. The activities of such bodies – or, for that matter, of individuals who seek the same ends – are, of course, highly contro-versial. One school of thought points to the demand for public protection against what is deemed unwholesome in leisure activity, a demand that mainly concerns commercial forms of leisure. But another school upholds the right of individuals to enjoy themselves in ways of their own choosing, provided that this does not interfere with the right of others to do the same.

The 'time famine'

In earlier and rural societies the term 'famine' most evidently refers to a shortage of food. In modern industrial societies there is usually enough food to go round – but not enough time. This felt shortage of time is most apparent among the middle class in the United States and Sweden, but is beginning to spread to equivalent groups in Britain. One of the best-known studies of this phenomenon is that of Staffan Linder,[20] and we may trace the main lines of his analysis and see how far they apply to contemporary British society.

The basic proposition is that a dwindling scarcity of goods entails an increasing scarcity of time. There is much evidence that people in advanced industrial societies live under the tyranny of the clock and that, in Linder's phrase, the 'harried leisure class' is growing. The affluent societies have largely become so because of huge gains in the output per head of material goods made possible by specialisation of labour and capital-intensive rather than labour-intensive methods of production. But the benefits of such methods have not been so apparent in the spheres of self and personal property maintenance. People still need time to maintain their own bodies: to sleep, eat and clean their teeth. The more goods and gadgets they have, the more time will have to be spent on buying and maintaining them.

The maintenance work of the housewife may be simplified by washing machines, and electric shavers may reduce the time spent by the husband on his morning toilet. But, when trying to assess the *time*, as opposed to the labour, saved, we must remember that the mechanical aids themselves require time for servicing and that they claim work time to earn money for their purchase. Also, the time it takes to get an appliance ready for use or to clean it after use may exceed the time it would take to do the job by hand. In either case, some part of what would otherwise be spent as leisure time is devoted to do-it-yourself work.

The implications of all this for leisure are twofold. With little or no reduction in work and self-maintenance time, and an increase in goods-maintenance time, there is less time for leisure. Furthermore, the same attitude which seeks to save time in work and non-work obligations spills over into an attempt to save time in leisure. Speeding up physical and mental operations in work leads logically to speeding up non-work obligations: food is thawed and heated rather than cooked, some people eat their lunch standing up, and many cannot spare the time for exercise to keep themselves healthy. Children are farmed out to nurseries; parents purchase exemption from giving them personal attention by pressing coins into their hands. At the other end of the life-cycle, only a few people will sacrifice the time needed to care adequately for the old and infirm.

The quality of leisure, too, is affected by the need to save time. Many forms of pleasure take time to enjoy properly, but increasingly attempts are made to skimp on them. A love affair takes time, as does learning to play a musical instrument or writing a poem. With good evidence, Geoffrey Godbey suggests that the practice of taking a mistress has largely died out because it is too time-consuming.[21] It has been replaced by the 'one nighter', lending support to the view that today's sexual promiscuity is primarily due to the desire to speed up the courtship process and to achieve intimacy in a very short period of time. To take another example, young people generally favour the kind of dancing which can be picked up quickly: they have psychologically, if not literally, no time to learn the intricate steps and routines of dances popular among the older generation.

The theme of a 'time famine', and its consequent effects on the quality of leisure experiences available to the more affluent members of advanced industrial societies, leads to a questioning of whether, and in what sense, we have made progress towards 'a society of leisure'. Godbey claims that what has increased, particularly during the last decade, is 'anti-leisure': activity which is undertaken compulsively, as a means to an end, from a perception of necessity, with a high degree of externally imposed constraints, with considerable anxiety, with a high degree of time consciousness and a minimum of personal autonomy.[22] This is not, of course, a picture of life characteristic of the majority of the population in the United States today, far less in Britain. But it applies to a significant and growing minority, and the dynamic of industrial capitalism is such that it is likely to spread in the future. In their recent study of work and leisure in the London region, Young and Willmott found that, at higher socio-economic levels, people brought something of the same sort of professionalism into their leisure as they did into their work, and that leisure often meant furious activity.[23] It is difficult to tell at what point anti-leisure will outstrip leisure, but that it may do so sooner rather than later or not at all appears increasingly likely.

Variations among industrial societies

In the previous section we noted that among industrial societies there are variations in the extent to which the material affluence and hence scarcity of time have affected the experience of and attitudes towards leisure. We may now consider the wider question of other possible variations among these societies in respect of leisure. Some commentators have used the concept of post-industrial society in this connection. Thus Dumazedier offers no precise definition of this type of society, but instead refers to a number of different descriptions of it: scientific-technical, cybernetic, a society of consumer goods, of universal education, and so on.[24] Provided one recognises that the transition from 'industrial' to 'post-industrial' societies is continuous rather than discrete, this distinction may be useful in analysing the comparative role of leisure in different societies.

Recently a factual basis has become available for comparing the amount of free time enjoyed by people in the twelve countries (not all industrial societies) taking part in the multi-national time budget study: East and West Germany, the Soviet Union, the United States, Bulgaria, Czechoslovakia, Hungary, Poland, Yugoslavia, Belgium, France and Peru.[25] It is not possible to summarise here the wealth of data on the amount of free time that people in various domestic, age and socio-economic categories claim to have, but it seems fair to say that the differences between countries are not dramatic. It should, however, be borne in mind that the study, though carefully planned, is open to a number of methodological criticisms. Time budgets depend on the memories and accurate recording of the individuals involved, and it is known that people tend to underestimate or omit activities which are considered immoral or of 'low status'. Also the refusal rate has in some cases been as high as 90 per cent.

Apart from whatever differences there may be between societies in amounts of time available for leisure and ways in which it is spent, there is also the question of possible different approaches taken to leisure and free time. Marie-France Lanfant, in a book not available in English translation,[26] has described some of these differences, and her main conclusions are summarised by Parry and Johnson.[27] There has, she claims, been a process of convergence between Marxist and liberal writers and between East and West concerning conceptual thinking about leisure and free time. The Marxists originally looked at free time in the context of the economic exploitation based on social class which was said to be the main feature of capitalism. They made efforts to demonstrate that very little genuinely free time was available to people in capitalist societies, and were pioneers of the time-budget approach. Liberal writers, on the other hand, sought to show that hours of work were falling in the West and used attitude surveys and impressionistic accounts to argue that the feeling of freedom and the actuality of choice was increasing.

According to Lanfant, there has recently been a blurring or merging of approaches to leisure in the East and West. This proposition may be tested against experience of leisure in the contemporary Soviet Union. Jeremy Azrael notes that, because of over-crowding and poor equipment, the average Soviet home cannot serve as the same sort of leisure centre as its American counterpart.[28] He does not deny that the Soviet citizen enjoys and even seeks exposure to 'culture', but he maintains that it is amusement which is sought rather than an opportunity for genuine recreation. A survey by Kharchev and Perfilyev shows that the majority of young people 'preferred to spend their free time at home or visiting relatives and friends' and that they 'spend a large part of their free time in the courtyards and streets'.[29] They also noted that some clubs and Palaces of Culture have to all intents and purposes been converted into movie houses, which seems to confirm Azrael's point about culture.

Leisure values, too, appear to be remarkably similar in the East and the West. Rosemarie Rogers concluded from her study in the Soviet Union that the most favoured leisure pursuits (in the sense of feeling that they were a 'good thing') were reading, attending the theatre, concerts, exhibitions or museums, and engaging in sports or arts activities.[30] Less favoured were radio listening, watching television and going to the cinema. Agreement on these norms was greater than on actual preferences for and exposure to the various leisure activities. In general, these findings confirm a remarkable similarity between the Soviet Union and the United States in normative and behaviour aspects of leisure, and it seems that any further comparison with Britain would emphasise similarities rather than differences.

REFERENCES

1   T. Burns, 'Leisure in Industrial Society', in M. A. Smith *et al.*, eds, *Leisure and Society in Britain* (Loudon, Allen Lane, 1973), p. 46.
2   J. Dumazedier, *Sociology of Leisure* (Amsterdam, Elsevier, 1974), p. 15.
3   K. Roberts, *Leisure* (London, Longman, 1970), p. 65.
4   T. McCormack, 'Politics and Leisure', *International Journal of Comparative Sociology*, September 1971.
5   J. Dumazedier, 'The Dynamics of Free Time or Leisure in Advanced Industrial Societies', *Lo Spettacolo* (Rome), September 1972.
6   Roberts, *op. cit.*, p. 10.
7   *Department of Employment Gazette*, January 1975.
8   M. Young and P. Willmott, *The Symmetrical Family* (London, Routledge, 1973), p. 113.
9   J. Child and B. Macmillan, 'Managers and their Leisure', in M. A. Smith *et al.*, eds, *op. cit.*
10   S. R. Parker, *The Future of Work and Leisure* (London, Paladin, 1972), p. 82.
11   N. Anderson and K. Ishwaran, *Urban Sociology* (London, Asia Publishing House, 1965), p. 175.
12   Labour Research Department, *The Two Nations: Inequality in Britain Today* (London, 1973), p. 20.
13   *The Sunday Times*, 20 May 1972.
14   M. Harrington, 'Leisure as the Means of Production', in L. Kolakowski and S. Hampshire, *The Socialist Idea: A Reappraisal* (London, Weidenfeld, 1974).
15   W. H. Auden, 'Culture and Leisure', *Ekistics*, November 1967, p. 419.
16   H. Entwistle, *Education, Work and Leisure* (London, Routledge, 1970).
17   R. Lynes, 'Time on Our Hands', *Harper's Magazine*, July 1958.
18   Burns, *op. cit.*, p. 45.
19   *Ibid.*, p. 46.
20   S. B. Linder, *The Harried Leisure Class* (New York, Columbia University Press, 1970).
21   G. Godbey, 'Anti-leisure and Public Recreation Policy', in S. R. Parker *et al.*, eds, *Sport and Leisure in Contemporary Society* (London, Polytechnic of Central London, 1975), p. 47.
22   *Ibid.*, p. 46.
23   Young and Willmott, *op. cit.*, p. 238.
24   Dumazedier, *op. cit.* (1974), p. 18.
25   A. Szalai, ed., *The Use of Time* (The Hague, Mouton, 1972).
26   M. F. Lanfant, *Theories du Loisir* (Paris, Presses Univ. de France, 1972).
27   N. C. A. Parry and D. Johnson, 'Sociology and Leisure', in S. R. Parker *et al.*, eds, *op. cit.*
28   J. R. Azrael, 'Notes on Soviet Urban Attitudes Toward Leisure', *Social Problems*, Summer 1961.
29   A. G. Kharchev and M. Perfilyev, 'A Sociologist's Notes: A Free Evening', in P. Hollander, ed., *American and Soviet Society* (Englewood Cliffs, N.J., Prentice-Hall, 1969).
30   R. Rogers, 'Normative Aspects of Leisure Time Behavior in the Soviet Union', *Sociology and Social Research*, July 1974.

Chapter 3

Variety of Leisure Experience

Our concern in this chapter is with the various ways in which people can experience leisure. There are many possible methods of classifying types of leisure, though most are less than comprehensive. Approaches and attitudes to leisure are conditioned by work values, producing either a reaction to work or forms of 'anti-leisure'. Leisure sub-cultures are apparent in the different ways in which people in broad social groups choose to spend their free time. To the individual, the meaning of leisure is often as a source of personal or shared-group identity, though the passive consumption of leisure may be a form of alienation from a more active involvement with social activities and concerns. We shall look at forms of leisure behaviour which represent either a conformist or 'square' attitude to existing institutions or a 'deviant' opposition to them, or both.

Classification of types of leisure

In Chapter 1 we briefly reviewed some definitions of leisure and some functions and meanings attached to the term. It is now appropriate to attempt a more detailed analysis. As Max Kaplan remarks, the problem is not to find classifications but to isolate those issues that seem to be most relevant for understanding behaviour.[1] He takes three such issues as examples, and builds from them six corresponding sub-categories of leisure experience:

(1) Do people relate to other *people as values*? Sociability, association.
(2) Do they prefer activities that are fixed by *rules and traditions*? Game, art.
(3) Do they seek to *go to the world* for direct and new experiences? Yes – movement, no – immobility.

Each of the first two categories has a set of opposites and any given leisure experience can partake of more than one of the six sub-categories. Thus there are solitary activities as well as sociable ones, creative or relatively free as well as rule-bound or tradition-bound ones. Games and art can be sociable or solitary and can (according to whether one engages in them as a performer or as a spectator) involve movement or immobility.

Kaplan's six sub-categories may be compared with two other ways of classifying types of leisure activity: one by Ray Maw[2] and the other in the Multi-National Time Budget Research Project.[3] This is done in Table 1.

Table 1   *Three classifications of types of leisure*

Kaplan	Maw	Time Budget
Sociability	Talking, Parties, etc.	Social Life, Conversation
Association	—	Organisations
Game	Sport and Active Play	Sports
Art	Theatre	Movies, Theatre, etc.
Movement	Dining and Drinking Out, Do-It-Yourself, Gardening, Driving for Pleasure	Walking
Immobility	Relaxing, Passive Play, TV, Radio, Reading, etc.	Resting TV, Radio, Reading
—	Hobbies	Hobbies

There is a good deal of equivalence of categories across the three sources: the Time Budget categories are more comprehensive, so it is not surprising that Kaplan's scheme has no obvious place for hobbies and that Maw does not explicitly allow for associational forms of leisure. Perhaps the most important point to make is that it would be extremely difficult to devise a classificatory scheme that did justice to all forms of leisure experience, neither over-simplifying the differences by having too few categories nor obscuring the underlying dimensions by having too many. We need to realise that almost any human activity – including the major ones which we shall consider in relation to leisure in Part Two – can provide leisure-like experiences for some people, depending on their circumstances and attitudes of mind.

Another way of approaching the classification of leisure experiences is in terms of functions that they serve for individuals: Joffre Dumazedier does this by distinguishing three functions, those of relaxation, diversion, and developing of the personality.[4] Rolf Meyersohn arrives at an expanded version of these functions by taking into account certain issues which face individuals.[5] (1) It is necessary for all of us to have intervals between bouts of work and other obligatory activities – hence leisure as rest, respite, recuperation. (2) We have a need for diversion, to gain pleasure from spectacles and performances of various kinds – leisure as entertainment. (3) Nevertheless, the dominant values in our society encourage us to seek achievements in all spheres of life and to be competent in what we do – leisure as self-realisation. (4) Finally (as if to question the material basis of many meanings attached to the term 'leisure') we may feel the need for spiritual renewal, difficult though this concept is to define and measure.

It is also possible to classify only part of the total range of leisure activities. Roger Caillois does this in what he calls four 'fundamental categories' of games. First, there is *agon*, signifying a group of competitive games in which a winner emerges from a contest involving the use of skill (football, chess). Second are games *alea*, based on decisions independent of the player, in which he has no control over the outcome (roulette, a lottery). Third, *mimicry* covers forms of play involving illusion and make-believe (theatre, carnival). Fourth, *ilinx* includes games producing a rapid whirling or falling movement, or a state of dizziness and disorder (acrobatics, tobogganing). Caillois emphasises that these types are not mutually exclusive: thus certain spectator sports (*agon*) are occasions for mimicry.

The decline of work values?

The important point from which to begin an explanation of leisure is in the way people themselves define the experience. If leisure were entirely a matter of time, if it were to be equated with 'free time', then it would be possible to be completely objective about it and to accept as leisure what people did during specified 'free' hours. But time free from obligations may not always *feel like* leisure, and leisure-like experiences may be possible during a space of time that is designated as 'work' or something other than leisure. This is to say, the situation is complicated by leisure's other dimension: that of activity. We cannot allocate specific activities to leisure or non-leisure. Of two men performing the same activity, say, playing golf or a musical instrument, one will be at leisure and the other earning a living. All leisure occupies a segment of time and consists of certain activities but is not reducible to these things. As Michael Smith puts it, leisure is closely linked to people's sense of enjoyment and freedom, their capacity for self-realisation and self-expression, the process of recreation and renewal, the possibility of choice.[6]

In Chapter 5 we shall deal with the relationship between leisure and work, both as social institutions and as segments of individual life.

As a prelude to this, we may examine some issues in the cultural context of both leisure and work. It is often asserted that, from being ascendant in the nineteenth century and the early part of the present century, work values have declined and been replaced by leisure values. How far is this true? In the previous chapter we examined critically the proposition that leisure now constitutes a separate and developing institution in its own right. We shall find that a similarly critical approach to propositions about the decline of work values is desirable.

If leisure has indeed taken over from work as a guiding principle of the essential values by which we live, then we should expect to see this reflected in the nature of leisure experiences, in so far as these are communicated to others or otherwise open to observation. Do we find a strong and developing set of leisure values – a world of play set against and at least to some extent counterbalancing the world of work? Certainly, as we have seen, there is the growth of the leisure industries, plus an increasing concern with planning and providing for leisure. Perhaps it is true that people generally are freer than they were – freer, that is, to consume a wider variety of leisure goods and services. But what of the real experience of leisure, the way it feels as a part of everyday life, the constraints upon it and the opportunities for personal growth afforded by it?

The sociologist *qua* sociologist is not in a position to answer this question. All he can do is to gather evidence about people's reported feelings, and seek to relate such evidence to empirical referents. Dumazedier sees leisure as having 'been introduced by means of a profound mutation of the being which means that a new relationship is established between the individual and his or her exterior nature, and the individual and his or her inner being. This results in leisure becoming the framework of a kind of cultural revolution.'[7] The clear implication of Dumazedier's extensive writings on leisure, despite his recent admission that post-industrial society 'will not be for everyone the society of free time',[8] is that leisure plays a bigger part in people's lives than formerly. Geoffrey Godbey disagrees, maintaining that what has increased, particularly during the last decade, is anti-leisure. 'By anti-leisure I refer to activity which is undertaken compulsively, as a means to an end, for a perception of necessity, with a high degree of externally composed constraints, with considerable anxiety, with a high degree of time consciousness, with a minimum of personal autonomy and which avoids self-actualization, authentication or finitude.'[9]

Given that people in North America, Sweden – and perhaps increasingly in Britain – display something of this approach to the use of their leisure time, the nature of what is experienced as 'leisure' is open to question. Perhaps we need to return, at least for some purposes, to the Aristotelean notion of leisure, to which, as Pierre Berton reminds us, the idea of 'using' time is foreign: 'leisure equals freedom'.[10] Without such an appreciation of its qualitative and cultural basis, it is easy to find a hollowness about leisure as a concept, as if it were only time to be filled.[11] As we shall see in more detail later in this book, the uses of leisure relate, often quite deeply, to the nature and conditions of work: there is a profound connection between the culture of a society – the whole quality of its arts, entertainments and thinking – and the general social and economic organisation.

Elite and mass culture

Industrial society is based on the growth of specialised economic and social organisations, including leisure organisations. One consequence of this division of life and labour is that man has become 'anomic' – exposed to conflicting values and a variety of reference groups.[12] Critics of this state of affairs claim that increasing numbers of people are becoming alienated both from the social institutions of which they are nominally members and from their 'true' identity. There is deep concern about the inner fate of the individual under the impact of the levelling powers of institutional and other organised forms of leisure activity.[13]

The relationship between culture and the socio-economic structure of society, like the relationship between work and leisure, is one of both opposition and extension. On one level, culture, being the broad effect of art, operates against the economic workaday structure of society. As Jeff Nuttall puts it, 'The economic structure works towards stasis centred around the static needs of man. It is centripetal. Culture forces change centred around the changing appetites of man. It is centrifugal.'[14]

But culture – whether expressed through literature, art, drama or radical criticism – is also deeply influenced by the structure and forms of social relationship characteristic of the society as a whole. Just as there are privileged and underprivileged classes or groups in respect of economic functions, so there are poles of meaning and experience to which individuals are encouraged to gravitate: poles which carry the admittedly over-simplified labels of elite and mass culture. The 'leisure class' which supported the high culture of the past has dwindled as a separate group, and political democracy and popular education have broken down the old upper-class monopoly of culture.[15] But, just as it is untrue to say that we no longer have a class-divided society because material standards of consumption have been generally raised, so it is untrue to claim that we no longer have an elite culture because even the rich consume some products of mass culture.

Alain Touraine refers to 'the distinction between active and passive leisure activities or, if one prefers, between elite and mass culture'.[16] It is arguable that to equate 'active' with 'elite' and 'passive' with 'mass' is to impose a false identification: the elite as those who are active, the mass as those who are passive. But Touraine seeks to justify the generalisation, and would no doubt claim that it is insightful rather than without exception. For him, 'the essential fact is that cultural activity is determined by the level of social participation, by the place occupied on the ladder of stratification'.[17] The wage-earners participate in mass culture by acquiring products and patronising entertainments; salary earners are open to 'cultural messages' which relate leisure to organisation and career objectives; only the top managers with no 'status anxiety' can engage in cultural activity for its own sake. However, Touraine is not pessimistic about mass society: he writes of the 'powerful forces of cultural manipulation' but he believes that an increasing number of people can 'escape some of the influences exercised over them and can act autonomously'.

Another and less optimistic view of cultural expressions and their influence on leisure experience is that of Erich Fromm. In a more critical evaluation of Touraine's passive mass culture, Fromm describes what he calls 'the *receptive* orientation, in which the aim is to receive, to "drink in", to have something new all the time, to live with a continuously open mouth, as it were'.[18] This alienated attitude to consumption is said to exist not only in the acquisition and consumption of commodities but also in the use of leisure time:

'If a man works without genuine relatedness to what he is doing, if he buys and consumes commodities in an abstractified and alienated way, how can he make use of his leisure time in an active and meaningful way? He always remains the passive and alienated consumer. He "consumes" ball games, moving pictures, newspapers and magazines, books, lectures, natural scenery, social gatherings. . . . Actually, he is not free to enjoy "his" leisure; his leisure-time consumption is determined by industry, as are the commodities he buys; his taste is manipulated, he wants to see and hear what he is conditioned to want to see and hear.'[19]

Fromm is not concerned with elite and mass culture in those terms: he contrasts the receptive orientation typical of capitalistic society with the productive orientation which he conceives as the active and creative relatedness of man to his fellow man, to himself and to nature. Both Touraine and Fromm agree that passive-mass-consumer culture is something to be escaped from rather than accepted – Touraine thinks this can be done on an individual basis, Fromm implies that a social revolution is necessary. There are no 'findings' available to us that will indicate which of these positions is more tenable or in line with reality. We can, however, get a better guide to the possibilities by looking more closely at the manifestations of culture in specific fields of leisure activity such as sport and art.

Sport in its organised form is a microcosm of society.[20] It has often been noted that sport has both a ritualistic and a dramatic aspect. The elements of ritual are due only partly to the rule-ordered and stereotyped nature of mass sporting events. They are more fundamentally to do with the socio-psychological functions served by ritual in any context: the rites of passage and of deference which mark off and deepen attachment to groups (teams) and the rites of intensification which 'unite the differentiated'.[21] As drama, a sports event is a play involving enjoyment and excitement; identification with hero characters (players) involves imagination and fantasy. It may be an exaggeration to claim, as does Rene Maheu, that 'spectator sports are the true theatre of our day',[22] but they are at least in the same tradition.

Sport, however, is also related to the prevailing values in our society, and there is substantial evidence that it operates as a means of social control. This applies particularly to the teaching of school sports. Sport as 'character training' was developed in the public schools and the idea that sport has 'educational value' is evident in the state schools today. As John Hargreaves shows, the central features of sport bear a close resemblance to consensual political values.[23] Sport is inherently competitive, and is therefore an effective mode of socialisation into the competitive mores of contemporary society. As a rule-governed competition, it encourages players to know and accept the rules of 'fair play' just as citizens are encouraged to accept that the rules of society are neutral and that everyone is equal before the law. And cultivation of the team spirit is good not only for the game but also for that form of economic behaviour which is regarded as in the country's interest.

Compared with sports, some forms of the arts present a greater challenge to the cultural *status quo*. The cinema, the theatre – and, more latterly, television – have functioned in part as powerful media of social criticism. Although, in respect of the arts generally, there are not two completely separate cultures, there is certainly a form of cultural stratification. John Clarke sums up the situation thus: 'the cultural division is between a dominant culture, which embraces most of the society and is subscribed to in one form or another, with varying degrees of commitment, by most of the members of society;

and the subordinated culture, which is more localised and limited, and yet extremely powerful'.[24] The key institution of the dominant ('bourgeois') culture is seen as conventional education, and examples of the subordinated culture include the institutions of organised labour such as the working men's clubs, though the shallow conformity in the working-class style of life has not been without criticism.[25]

Whether we are referring to sport, the arts or other forms of leisure, arguments for and against the proposition that there are 'two cultures' are difficult to avoid. One can counter the proposition by drawing attention to the essential unity of culture or to its multiplicity. We shall return to this subject when dealing below with 'square' and 'deviant' leisure.

The search for identity

An approach to leisure behaviour which seeks to understand it in terms only of the overt activities engaged in is insufficient. What counts is the meaning attached to the activity – which is why the same activity can be leisure or not leisure. As Orrin Klapp succinctly puts it, the urgent question is not What can I do? but Who can I be?[26]

Identity-seeking behaviour is too widespread to be categorised as 'abnormal'; it is a symbolic problem of society rather than a psychological trait of the individual. Some identities are, of course, sought and found in the work sphere, but with the de-skilling and routinisation of much modern employment this is not possible for many people. So the aim of having fun increasingly challenges and supplants the aim of having creative work. The values spread by 'education for leisure' and the opportunities created by the leisure industries mean that the modest aim of enabling people to enjoy themselves is frequently achieved. But there is a growing cult of fun which goes deeper than that. Beyond the notion that fun is a right thing to have, there is what Klapp calls the new romanticism: the right to find oneself, to realise oneself, through fun as 'peak experience'.[27]

Klapp lists eight ways (with examples) in which play or fun activities can become cult-like, that is, can give people the feeling of having supreme moments, the best there is, kicks or ecstasies: (1) ordeals by which one finds new capacities within oneself (mountain climbing, sky-diving); (2) fellowship with an elect who have a mystique not shared with outsiders (venerated musical or other performers); (3) vestment change (costume for some sports); (4) intensity of stimulation leading to ecstasy (dancing to a hypnotic beat); (5) interest so strong that one 'invests' oneself (almost any art or hobby can lend itself to this); (6) spectators' vicarious excitement (followers of entertainers and sports stars); (7) audience hero worship (as of the body beautiful); and (8) self-abandonment in orgy (nude parties). Some of these activities are at best frowned upon by conventional society and at worst are anti-social. Some of the examples are ephemeral but the themes themselves are more durable and not to be ignored in any study of leisure experiences.

Ralph Glasser has come to a conclusion similar to that of Klapp: that leisure choices reflect the stages that the search for a desirable identity has reached in people or groups.[28] But Glasser, unlike Klapp, stresses the role of the persuasion process in the identity search. From his depth survey into shopping motivations he concludes that the primary aim is not to make purchases but to perceive and to re-affirm a satisfactory identity. The persuasion process of advertising and marketing is designed to answer the need for reassurance as to what is the desirable identity to pursue – the 'executive' house or the 'director' suit. This process, according to Glasser, extends also to leisure. Because leisure is the area of life where more or less free choices are available, they reflect the stages that the search for a desirable identity has reached in people or groups. Clearly the idea that identity-search prompts *all* leisure choices would be to overstate the case, but that it plays a prominent part seems undeniable.

'Square' and 'deviant' leisure

The theme of identity-search leads logically to questions about the relationship of leisure choices to needs to conform with or to rebel against conventional social forms. Klapp sees the relationship between identity-search and unconventionality as follows.

'Once "fun" stops being what people do for amusement or relaxation from work and becomes part of a search for identity, it provides a basis for a theory of why people deviate. The stress is [on] . . . what people do who are bored, want to have more meaning in their lives, and make certain choices in their leisure. This search for meaningful fun, for "kicks", leads from banal forms of amusements to realizing ones: it takes the seeker to offbeat experiences, cults, poses and bizarre drama.'[29]

Klapp's hypothesis is that 'squares' have a firm identity and are satisfied with the opportunities of the *status quo*, whereas those with identity problems feel cheated by the *status quo* and disdainful of its opportunities, and hence search for a new identity along the 'trail of kicks'. From this point of view, much of what we call deviance is essentially a cultic quest 'to find highest experience and new identity among those who feel cheated'. The squares are different in goal rather than motivation: they happen to 'find their kicks within the respectable order of family, church, school, and business' – and, one might add, in suitably self-confirming and conventional forms of leisure activity.

It is instructive to look at those leisure activities which can take square or deviant forms according to the goals of the participants. Tourism is one example: as Erik Cohen notes, it 'connotes a change from routine, something different, strange, unusual or novel, an experience not commonly present in the daily life of the traveller'.[30] The change from routine can function as a refresher for the return to routine – or as a releaser of inhibitions pent up by routine. In the one case the tourist activities will be moderately conventional and probably law-abiding; in the other case, the alien environment may be the setting for more extreme, violent and perhaps illegal conduct. A quite different example of square and deviant forms of the same basic activity is provided by urban 'sensory walks', in which participants are asked to stop and listen or look. The conventional walk, drawing attention to 'desirable' features of the man-made environment, can be good public relations for the local authority. On the other hand a 'counter culture' walk, laid around some of the worst blunders of the planners, can become a revolutionary activity.[31]

Visiting public houses is a form of leisure activity, mostly square but with deviant overtones, which has often been underrated as an area of study. As Malcolm Wilders shows, pub visiting is by far the most popular social activity among young people, and it accounts for something like 30 per cent of the total turnover of leisure industries.[32] The social environment created in the pub helps people to relax from the physical and psychological restrictions of workaday life. The pub is also an important leisure centre, often providing – as well as the more traditional games of darts, dominoes and billiards – less conventional forms of entertainment such as striptease, drag, and go-go dancing. Historically the pubs have been associated with illegal activities such as boxing, ratting and dog fighting. Today the activities are seldom illegal, but they often have the flavour of permissiveness and release of inhibitions.

Some forms of leisure are 'square' in the sense of reinforcing work values, providing amusement without insight and pleasure without disturbance. Other forms of leisure embody values – Jock Young calls these 'subterranean'[33] – contrary to those which regulate conventional society. Short-term hedonism opposes deferred gratification, spontaneity is valued above planning future action, and so on. A relevant concept is that of the 'underground' which, like leisure itself, defies definition but which is said by one exponent to be a mixture of new cultural idiom, novel form of entertainment, drug sub-culture and quasi-religious cult.[34] From one point of view, the whole phenomenon of the 'underground' can be seen as a complex of legal and illegal business enterprises. There are the more or less 'respectable' leisure industries catering for the non-squares as well as the squares, and the traffickers in drugs who prey unlawfully on human weakness. On the borders of these two, within the law but often regarded as morally disreputable, are a mixed bunch of entrepreneurs who provide what Jeremy Sandford calls synthetic fun.[35] People who do not like the real world can be sold 'fun' experiences in which they can forget and replace it by a dream world. With synthetic fun you don't have to give very much of yourself.

REFERENCES

1 M. Kaplan, *Leisure in America* (New York, Wiley, 1960), p. 25.
2 R. Maw, 'Construction of a Leisure Model', *Official Architecture and Planning*, August 1969.
3 A. Szalai, ed., *The Use of Time* (The Hague, Mouton, 1972).
4 J. Dumazedier, *Toward a Society of Leisure* (London, Collier-Macmillan, 1967).
5 R. Meyersohn, 'Leisure', in A. Campbell, ed., *The Human Meaning of Social Change* (New York, Russell Sage Foundation, 1972).
6 M. A. Smith, Introduction to *Leisure and Society in Britain* (London, Allen Lane, 1973), p. 7.
7 Dumazedier, *op. cit.*
8 *Ibid.*
9 G. Godbey, 'Anti-leisure and Public Recreation Policy', in S. R. Parker *et al.*, eds, *Sport and Leisure in Contemporary Society* (London, Polytechnic of Central London, 1975).
10 P. Berton, *The Smug Minority* (Toronto, McClelland and Stewart, 1968), p. 77.
11 R. Williams, 'Towards a Socialist Society', in P. Anderson and R. Blackburn, eds, *Towards Socialism* (London, Fontana, 1965), p. 395.
12 S. R. Parker and M. A. Smith, 'Work and Leisure', in R. Dubin, ed., *Handbook of Work, Organization and Society* (Chicago, Rand McNally, 1976).
13 L. Lowenthal, in B. Rosenberg and D. M. White, eds, *Mass Culture* (Glencoe, Free Press, 1957), p. 47.
14 J. Nuttall, *Bomb Culture* (London, MacGibbon & Kee, 1968), p. 8.
15 D. Macdonald, in Rosenberg and White, eds, *op. cit.*, p. 59.
16 A. Touraine, *The Post-industrial Society* (London, Wildwood House, 1974), p. 206.
17 *Ibid.*, p. 208.
18 E. Fromm, *The Sane Society* (London, Routledge, 1956), p. 136.
19 *Ibid.*

D

20 J. Hargreaves, 'The Political Economy of Mass Sport', in Parker *et al.*, eds, *op. cit.*, p. 60.

21 J. A. Mangan, 'Physical Education as a Ritual Process', in J. A. Mangan, ed., *Physical Education and Sport: Sociological and Cultural Perspectives* (Oxford, Blackwell, 1973), p. 88.

22 R. Maheu, 'Sport and Culture', in Mangan, ed., *op. cit.*, p. 172.

23 Hargreaves, *op. cit.*, p. 60.

24 J. Clarke, 'Framing the Arts: The Role of Cultural Institutions', paper presented to the Symposium on Sport and Culture in Contemporary Society, London, January 1975.

25 R. Hoggart, *The Uses of Literacy* (London, Chatto & Windus, 1957).

26 O. Klapp, *Collective Search for Identity* (New York, Holt, Rinehart, 1969), p. x.

27 *Ibid.*, p. 185.

28 R. Glasser, 'Leisure and the Search for a Satisfying Identity', in Smith *et al.*, eds, *op. cit.*, p. 60.

29 Klapp, *op. cit.*, p. 200.

30 E. Cohen, 'Who is a Tourist? A Conceptual Clarification', *Sociological Review*, November 1974.

31 B. Goodey, *Urban Walks and Town Trails* (Birmingham, Centre for Urban and Regional Studies, 1975).

32 M. G. Wilders, 'Some Preliminary Discussions on the Sociology of the Public House', in Parker *et al.*, eds, *op. cit.*

33 J. Young, 'The Hippie Solution', in I. and C. Taylor, eds, *Politics and Deviancy* (Harmondsworth, Penguin, 1973).

34 P. Fryer, 'A Map of the Underground', *Encounter*, October 1967.

35 J. Sandford, *Synthetic Fun* (Harmondsworth, Penguin, 1967).

Chapter 4

Leisure in the Life-Cycle

In this chapter we shall look at the role of leisure in the lives of individuals at various ages and in different family circumstances. First we shall examine the ways in which children experience play as leisure, paying particular attention to sex, age, social class and cultural differences. Our understanding of leisure during the period of youth depends on how we view the process of adolescence, and there are various theories to guide us here. During adult life there are changes taking place in most individuals' family responsibilities which affect their experience of and attitudes toward leisure. Finally, in the 'third age', there are special problems for both men and women who have to cope with a period at the end of their lives which is sometimes too easily thought of as 'all leisure'.

Children, play and leisure

It is doubtful whether we can sensibly use the concept of leisure at all for pre-school children, since time for them has not become institutionally divided between obligatory activity (at school) and non-obligatory activity.[1] For school children the notion of leisure becomes more appropriate, although the choice of leisure pursuits is normally restricted by parents and by the usually limited amount of pocket money children are given to spend. For pre-adolescent children the term 'play' has normally been used to describe activities which there is no obligation to undertake and which serve as ends in themselves – what for other groups we would call 'leisure'.[2] In practice, the play and leisure of pre-adolescent children amount to much the same set of activities, since such children generally play in their leisure time.

There are three broad types of theory about play which are relevant when considering the question of children and leisure: physiological, biological and psychological.[3] *Physiological* theories are mainly in terms of the expenditure of surplus energy (Herbert Spencer saw parents as providing for the basic needs of their young, whose energies had consequently to be expended on purposeless activities) or recreation (Lazarus believed that when a child is tired he can recuperate by expending energy on vigorous play). As the Childs remark, these physiological theories fail to explain most of the variations in play behaviour.

Biological theories divide mainly into the concepts of pre-practice play and recapitulation. Karl Groos defined play as the 'generalized impulse' to practise those instincts necessary for survival in adult life and thus, unlike Spencer, he viewed play as highly purposeful. Stanley Hall argued that at each stage of development the child re-enacted the experiences of his race at a defined stage in its history (thus children climbing trees recapitulate the ape stage in man's evolution). Of these theories, there is something to be said for Groos, especially in relation to children in pre-industrial societies, but little to be said for Hall.

Psychological explanations of children's play are mostly associated with Sigmund Freud and Jean Piaget. Freud saw play as having two main functions: the re-enactment of unpleasant events in order to master them ('repetition compulsion') and the modification of events in play as one would like them in reality ('wish fulfilment'). For Piaget, play was similar to learning and imitation, and featured the process of assimilation – digesting and integrating cultural materials and signals in order to make them the child's own. Again, while these theories account to some extent for children's motivation to play and their attitudes to adults and other children, they cannot cope with variations in play behaviour which are found in practice.

Some of the major variables which help to explain differences in children's play are those of sex, age, social class and culture. Many writers on children's play have noted the effects of sex differences. Some have discussed the different activities enjoyed by boys and girls, while others have singled out their different ways of playing. In the United States greater emphasis is given to achievement in the upbringing of boys, and American schoolboys play more games of physical skill.[4] With girls there is more emphasis on obedience, and they tend to play more games of strategy. However, recent evidence is that girls are increasingly coming to prefer what were formerly boys' activities. Thus traditionally male games such as baseball and camping today show less marked differences between the sexes. The change represents not so much a convergence between the play roles of the sexes as an expansion in the scope of girls' leisure activities.

At different ages boys and girls tend to prefer different types of play. These may be divided into physical (including games of skill), creative and imaginative. A study by Elizabeth Child showed that girls took part in all three types, though at different ages.[5] At about three years their play is mainly creative, for example, painting. Later, imaginative play increases, and from six to twelve years physical play is popular. In contrast, boys of all ages from three to twelve took part in physical activities most of all, with creative play second and imaginative play a poor third. Other studies show that children of both sexes with high IQs tend more often to engage in imaginative play.

Social class has a significant effect on type of play. The two main factors here are availability of play space and style of upbringing. Working-class children, as compared with middle-class children, generally have less play space inside the home and poorer facilities in their neighbourhood, so they more often play in the streets. The restrictiveness of an urban environment is particularly evident if children live in tower blocks, since they often have to make a considerable journey to the play area below. This is most unfortunate for pre-school children, since there is often little room indoors for them to play, and parents are unwilling to let them go outside on their own.

Style of upbringing or socialisation, which is linked with social class, also affects children's play. Although style of socialisation – strict or permissive, concerned more with discipline or with freedom – may vary from time to time within broad class groups, most children will be subject to parental influence which encourages one type of play rather than another. Working-class parents are likely to encourage their children to fight their own battles and thus to exhibit more overt aggression in their play. By contrast, children of middle-class parents are more likely to have their disputes arbitrated by their parents and to play with less apparent aggression in their own houses or gardens. Attendance at grammar or secondary modern school, which is correlated with class membership, has been found to result in differences in reading habits, club membership, and favourite activities outside school.[6]

Perhaps the most pervasive differences between types of children's play are because of the different cultures in which they are raised. Roberts and Sutton-Smith have put forward a 'conflict-enculturation' hypothesis to account for cross-cultural variations in play.[7] In societies which stress success as an important goal, children will play games of physical skill and use success in these games to assuage their anxiety about achievement. In these cases the basis of involvement in games is the need for relief from inner tensions which the socialisation process has brought about. Children in other cultures have a quite different set of motivations to play instilled in them. Thus the play of Hopi Indian children in general imitates the activities of adults: the girls play house and the boys build imitation corrals.[8]

Adolescents and leisure

The periods of childhood and of full adult status are separated by something called 'adolescence', though other nouns for this period of life include 'teenager', 'youth', 'young person', and so on. In some cultures, this period is short or even non-existent: individuals pass more or less straight from childhood to adulthood. Even in our own society, adolescence may be said to last longer for the middle class than for the working class. To understand the role of leisure at this stage in the life-cycle it will be helpful to bear in mind the three perspectives on adolescence suggested by Cyril Smith: as a period of socialisation during which the knowledge and attitudes appropriate to certain adult roles are internalised; as a period of various transitions in status and role; and as 'youth culture' having an autonomous influence which may conflict with adult values.[9]

During the period of adolescence the individual is socialised into leisure habits and attitudes through two main agencies: his family, and other institutions (chiefly schools and voluntary organisations) with which he comes into contact. The influence on a young person's leisure that his family has will depend on a number of factors, among which being in or out of full-time education and living with or apart from parents are two of the most important. A boy or girl at school or college and living with parents is subject to a considerable limitation of his or her leisure activities. While modern parents tend to feel the obligation to let their teenage non-earning children choose their own friends, the amount of pocket money allowed determines the possibilities of turning free time into leisure, at least of the consuming kind. A young person who is either living away from his parents or has a job (or both) is in a much better position to enjoy a wide choice of leisure activities and be relatively free from adult supervision of these. For most urban and financially independent youngsters the processes of dating and courtship take place in an atmosphere of commercialised recreation, over which parents have comparatively little influence.[10]

As we shall see in more detail in subsequent chapters, both educational and religious institutions play a part – though probably a decreasing one – in socialising young people into leisure habits and attitudes. To 'reach' young people, such institutions (including civic and other organisations aiming to cater to the needs or solve the problems of youth) have to effect a compromise between the 'fun' expectations of their clients and the more 'serious' expectations of their leaders. Some of the best work is being done where the gap between these two sets of expectations is least.

The second, transitional perspective on adolescence directs our attention to the successive small shifts in status and role which help to explain why juvenile behaviour so often appears uncertain, and the young person at a loss as to how he should behave. Progression from primary to secondary school and perhaps university involves successive improvements in status which normally carry with them greater command over resources and greater freedom of movement. Whereas the 'socialisation' perspective lays emphasis on the change in parental supervision when the young person enters employment, the 'transitional' perspective is more concerned with actual changes in the pattern of life and leisure. Towards the end of his school life the student will be under increasing pressures of competition for examination success and for entry into higher education, which will limit the time available for leisure.

For a young person who does not enter higher education, starting work full-time usually means much less time available for leisure. He is likely to set off for work earlier than he did for school and return later, probably more fatigued. Although his weekends will not be much affected, his holidays will be much shorter. To compensate for this, he is likely to have a sharp increase in income, making it possible to exercise more choice in leisure activities. Whether or not they go out to work, girls usually have a greater obligation to perform household duties than boys. Surveys show that teenage girls less often go out in the evenings than boys, though this difference is less marked in the later years of adolescence. There is also a social class difference: 'adolescent daughters of middle-class working mothers engage in much organized and unorganized leisure activity. . . . By contrast the daughters of lower-class working mothers report heavy home responsibilities and fewer leisure activities.'[11]

The third perspective on adolescent leisure is that of youth culture. Wherever young people have gathered together, apart from adults, they have tended to develop their own style of life, and the marked segregation of adolescent boys in working-class communities has produced the typical 'corner boy' culture. This segregation is now more common among all classes, and the pattern is shared by girls as well as boys. The expansion of the mass media has made it possible for the young to achieve a symbolic unity which does not need (though clearly is enhanced by) physical association. At the same time, adolescence is a period when the individual's involvement in family life is weak. In deciding how to use their spare time, young people in contemporary society are much more strongly influenced by the views of their peers than by those of their parents.[12] They are keen to develop new tastes, and they are willing to experiment, with the result that their leisure is extremely colourful and varied in contrast to the more stable and conventional pursuits of their elders.

Youth culture is closely identified with the world of entertainment and, more recently, with protest. Indeed, the two are linked, since some entertainers have become leading figures in social protest. The emergence of youth culture has led not only to commercial exploitation of this popular market, but has also presented a more fundamental challenge to the nature of industrial society by stimulating both protest and withdrawal movements. Protest has been especially concerned with race relations, but more recently also with nostalgia for a simpler and purer way of life in the communes. David Marsland sees youth culture as to some extent 'the necessary structural matrix of contemporary counter-cultural developments, and the seedbed of structural transformation to a new societal type'.[13] Youth culture has changed the character of 'pop' music and entertainment for adult audiences, and has altered clothing and hairstyles for age groups other than teenagers. However, the impact of the leisure styles of the young upon their elders should not be overestimated. Adults still form the larger part of the market for most forms of entertainment, and it is only with their support that these remain economically viable.

Leisure in adult life

Between the pre-employment 'first age' of childhood and adolescence and the 'third age' of retirement there is a substantial period of the life-cycle during which most adults are either working for a living or raising a family or both. There are exceptions to this broad generalisation – some adolescents and some persons beyond retirement age have a paid occupation – but for most of us the adult years from about twenty to sixty-five are more active than those before or later.

As Max Kaplan points out, a static view of the family is being increasingly discarded in realistic studies, including those of leisure.[14] 'The family' is many families as changes take place in the ages of the children, father's career or mother's work in the home and outside it. Consequently, we may review the experience of leisure by individuals at different adult ages and with varying responsibilities to other members of the family.

When dealing with a span of the life-cycle which embraces forty or more years, age is clearly a factor influencing changes in patterns and preferences for leisure activities. But chronological age is not by itself enough to explain all the differences. We need to take into account also that at any given age some people will be married and some single, and that some of the former will have no children, some young children, and some older children. The concept which includes all four dimensions – age, sex, marital status and children – has been called 'domestic age'. Researchers have found this concept useful in analysing and interpreting the results of surveys into leisure behaviour, and we shall find it similarly useful in summarising some of their results.

In 1965-6 a major leisure survey was carried out in a sample of urban areas in Britain, which provided much data on the recreational patterns of domestic age groups.[15] Although for the sample as a whole television viewing ranked as the most time-consuming leisure occupation, this was not so throughout the life-cycle. Among young single people (aged 15-22) the greatest emphasis was given to physical recreation. In fact for young men this continued as their outstanding leisure interest into early married life, and it was only when they became fathers that it fell to second place below television. Changes in leisure habits took place more swiftly among women: at marriage their participation in physical recreation dropped to fourth place below crafts and hobbies, television and social activities. For men, gardening, decorating and other do-it-yourself tasks became significant only after marriage. At 46-60, after their children had grown up, men tended to spend fewer leisure periods watching television, and there were signs of a slight revival of interest in physical recreation at this time. Women's crafts and hobbies (mainly knitting) were most often mentioned as chief leisure activities by married women between the ages of 23 and 45. At all ages, women mentioned social activities more frequently than men.

Another, smaller study concentrated on the leisure activities of the 17-32 age group and in one community just north of London.[16] It confirmed some of the findings of the larger survey and added others. Single people were found to take part in a much wider variety of activities outside the home than married people, and it is when they are single that there exists the greatest degree of similarity and equality in the leisure practices and preferences of the sexes. Social class had a bearing on leisure behaviour within each of the domestic age groups: for example, more people from white-collar and professional backgrounds participated in formal clubs, groups and organisations of all kinds than did those from blue-collar backgrounds. The researchers believe that their findings lend support to the picture of a well-defined and somewhat conventional pattern of leisure activities in the community studied. These are said to arise in the context of the life-cycle rather than being caused by any new factors which obtain today but were non-existent in the past.

Let us look more closely at the experience of leisure at various stages of the 'second age'. In recent decades the age of marriage has become lower and many more young couples find themselves parents in their early twenties than used to be the case. Before they were married, the young couple probably spent much of their free time together. Much tension may result if the young husband wants to spend most of his leisure time with friends from his single days.[17]

Equally, the young bride may want to spend all her spare time with her mother. More importantly, a young couple's decisions on how to spend their leisure will be partly determined by whether or not the wife is working. If the desire to start buying a house is the main reason for the wife working, then leisure expenditure will probably take second place. Other young couples who are content with modest accommodation may wish to spend more on leisure, including perhaps expensive holidays.

Parenthood brings about quite dramatic changes in the leisure habits of young people.[18] Their domestic responsibilities increase, with the result that the amounts of time and money available for leisure interests diminish. Such free time as is left tends to be spent in the home, and pursuits previously centred upon the peer group are often dropped. Few new leisure interests are acquired after marriage, with the exception of gardening, an interest which is consistent with a home-centred life. Marriage counsellors are concerned that some young married people are so tied down by small children that they practically become prisoners in their own homes, never getting out together in the evening and losing many of their former friends and interests. To some extent, babysitting – whether cooperative among a group of mothers, paid, or volunteered by grandparents – is an answer to this problem, but it is one that is not available to all couples.

As people grow into middle age and their children leave home, the domestic responsibilities of the couple become lighter. Household chores are less demanding, and more money is available for leisure. During this phase of life, leisure interests might be expected to be rejuvenated and people to engage in more activities outside the home. For the wife, in particular, release from the obligations of parental responsibility provides an impressive amount of free time.[19] Actually (as noted in the surveys) very little increase in participative leisure takes place. Some people do develop an active interest in community-based organisations, such as the church and civic associations, during their middle years, but this is not typical. The general trend is for leisure interests and activities to become increasingly restricted with age, despite decreased responsibilities.

Kenneth Roberts offers two explanations for this decline in leisure interests.[20] One is that during middle life the individual's physical and mental vigour declines, which may account for a reluctance to cultivate new interests. People may feel no inclination to do more than drift along in the routine to which they have become accustomed during their earlier years of married life. The second possible explanation is that so many of the leisure industries aim to capture the interest of younger age groups: an adolescent image has become attached to the ideas of having fun and seeking amusement, an image with which older people are reluctant to identify. Roberts suggests that it is probably this combination of social inhibitions and a lack of personal inclination that accounts for the widespread failure of people to fill their free time with new interests once their family responsibilities have diminished.

In the previous paragraphs we have been discussing the situation of married people. We must not, however, forget the substantial minorities of single people, including those who do not remarry. In terms of financing their leisure, single people are generally the lucky ones. They can afford more expensive holidays and more frequent outings than married couples on the same income. But many single men and women suffer from loneliness in their leisure hours, which in some cases results in neurotic conditions and even suicide.[21] This is particularly true in big cities, where life can be alien and impersonal. Just getting away from the city is not always a solution. Many single persons, especially women, take their loneliness with them on solitary holidays – or they may prefer to immerse themselves in work, including voluntary work, rather than face the emptiness of 'play' leisure.

Leisure and the elderly

Owing to improved medical science and social welfare, more people are living past retirement age, and for longer periods, than formerly. The elderly are often thought of as having a great deal of leisure, but only because it is assumed that they are no longer working and are in reasonably good health. Both these assumptions, however, are untrue for significant minorities of older people. Cross-cultural research in Britain, the United States and Denmark shows that between 24 and 31 per cent of men are still working at seventy, and between 15 and 19 per cent at seventy-five.[22] Other studies show that some 5 per cent of the elderly are in residential homes or hospitals, and the proportion who are either bedridden or housebound is 8 to 13 per cent.[23]

Health and mobility have an important effect on both the amount of leisure available to the elderly and the quality of its enjoyment. Satisfying use of leisure cannot substitute for poor health, lost family and friends, or an inadequate pension. Nor can it take the place of the feelings of usefulness and purposefulness which are probably the greatest needs of the aged.[24] For those in good health and able to move about freely, retirement can bring new opportunities to take up, or have more time for, a wide range of leisure pursuits. But for the elderly who are not in good health the problem of filling the empty hour is partly solved in that things take longer to do anyway. A report on a study of the handicapped and impaired showed that elderly men frequently had to give up participating in sports and gardening: elderly women most often had to give up handicrafts, walking and shopping.[25] The picture emerging from this study was one of a population with above-average amounts of disposable time but frustrated physically, mentally, environmentally and financially in its enjoyment of this extra free time.

Retired persons as a whole face the problem of what to do with extra time available. The problem particularly affects men, since women may well find that retirement from their job or from responsibilities connected with their own children is filled to some extent by activities connected with their grandchildren. There is a considerable difference between the social classes in the impact of retirement and the ways in which it is coped with. Men in professional and senior management occupations are often able to continue some form of work after official retirement age; this is less often possible for those in manual and many business occupations. Middle-class older women are more likely than working-class women to be already members of one or more voluntary organisations, and unless they have a paid occupation which ends at an arbitrary age they will not notice much change in their lives.

So far as participation in leisure activities is concerned, the process of withdrawal which we saw as frequently starting in middle life tends to continue into old age. This is no doubt due in some cases to changed financial position: some elderly people have to stop going out to places of entertainment or other events because they cannot afford it. There is some suggestion that hobby activities tend to increase after age fifty, but after the early seventies, with the diminution of sensory functions, they decrease again.[26] The major survey quoted earlier shows that the pattern of leisure of the elderly differs from that of younger people in several marked respects.[27] Whether in full-time employment or not, men aged 61+ spend more time on gardening, while among the retired group park visits and walks increase sharply. Single women aged 61+ spend much more time on social activities than do other women.

At present there are more than 7,000 social clubs for elderly people in England and Wales.[28] They vary from monthly socials held in a church hall to quite elaborately equipped day centres. The clubs themselves are not always welcomed by elderly people. Less than 7 per cent of old people attend a club in any given week, and it has been estimated that only 15–20 per cent of those entitled to use the clubs ever do so.[29] The clubs are generally more popular with women than with men, and men more often prefer clubs unrestricted by age. The question of whether clubs are a good thing is part of a broader issue of whether active leisure is something to be encouraged in preference to passive leisure. While there is every reason to seek to provide more adequate facilities for those who wish to take part in club activities, it is questionable whether people who show no signs of needing more social contact should be pressured to 'join in'.

Although the question of leisure for the elderly should by no means be identified with the question of adjustment to retirement, there are substantial grounds for seeking to understand the changing content and functions of leisure in the context of changed role-status on retirement. One of the foremost contributions to thinking in this area has been the 'disengagement theory' of Cumming and Henry. According to this theory,

'Ageing is an inevitable mutual withdrawal or disengagement resulting in decreased interaction between the ageing and others in the social system to which he belongs. The process may be initiated by the individual or by others in the situation. The ageing person may withdraw more markedly from some classes of people while remaining relatively close to others. His withdrawal may be accompanied from the outset by an increased preoccupation with himself; certain institutions in society may make this withdrawal easy for him.'[30]

The theory has led to a large number of research studies, some of which support it while others refute it. It has been extensively criticised, chiefly on the grounds that there is no reason to suppose that its propositions apply outside contemporary United States culture. It has also been suggested that, though it may be an adequate description of ageing as experienced by many fairly healthy and economically secure old people, it is not acceptable as a picture of ageing among other important groups of old people, such as the poor, the housebound or the extremely isolated.[31] The concept of 'activity within disengagement' has been suggested by Streib and Schneider to account for the trend and counter-trend.[32] They divide such activity into two main categories: the leisure role (which involves seeing the later years of life as 'leisure years') and the citizenship-service role (programmes by private and governmental agencies, including activity as foster grandparents and manning 'dial-a-friend' services).

We need to appreciate the extent to which the disengagement theory in particular, and the prevailing ideas about retirement in general, are class-based. It is significant that Marion Crawford found a *change* rather than a cessation of anticipated involvement after retirement by most groups.[33] Middle-class men in her study anticipated less interaction as friend and worker and more as leisure-time-user; working-class men felt the same, apart from substituting 'parent' for 'friend'. Middle-class women anticipated less interaction as worker and more as leisure-time-user; working-class women anticipated less interaction as neighbour and worker and more as parent. There is thus no question of 'disengagement' for most working-class women. Their lives have been embedded in an extended family and neighbourhood network, and they have probably never thought about separate activities or time called 'leisure'. But for other elderly women and most elderly men there is a real problem to be faced after the involuntary loss of one role and the difficulty of finding another.

A framework for analysis of change

To the extent that static categories such as age, sex and marital status are insufficient for understanding people's leisure behaviour and values, a framework is required that is amenable to the analysis of change and variation. The Rapoports have explored the utility of the family life-cycle framework for this purpose.[34] Individuals change their preoccupations, interests and activities as they develop in the course of their own life-cycle and as they move through social roles in relation to the family life-cycle and family structure (we shall deal more fully with leisure and the family in Chapter 6). Particular preoccupations may be present all through the life-cycle, but they often tend to become more salient at certain of its phases. Interests are formed, sustained or changed by the interaction between an individual's preoccupations and his social environment, at any or all of the stages of his life-cycle.

REFERENCES

1 E. and J. Child, 'Children and Leisure', in M. A. Smith *et al.*, eds, *Leisure and Society in Britain* (London, Allen Lane, 1973), p. 135.
2 A. Giddens, 'Notes on the Concepts of Play and Leisure', *Sociological Review*, March 1964.
3 E. and J. Child, *op. cit.*, pp. 136–8.
4 R. R. Sears *et al.*, *Patterns of Child-rearing* (New York, Harper, 1957).
5 E. and J. Child, *op. cit.*, pp. 142–3.
6 M. Stewart, 'The Leisure Activities of Grammar School Children', *British Journal of Educational Psychology*, vol. 40, 1970.
7 M. Roberts and B. Sutton-Smith, 'Child Training and Game Involvement', *Ethnology*, April 1962.
8 S. A. Queen and R. W. Habenstein, *The Family in Various Cultures* (Philadelphia, Lippincott, 1974, 4th edn), p. 59.
9 C. S. Smith, 'Adolescence', in Smith *et al.*, eds, *op. cit.*
10 W. Waller, *The Family – A Dynamic Interpretation* (New York, Dryden, 1951).
11 W. J. Goode, *The Family* (Englewood Cliffs, Prentice-Hall, 1964), p. 76.

12   K. Roberts, *Leisure* (London, Longman, 1970), p. 45.
13   D. Marsland, 'Youth and Leisure', in S. Parker *et al.*, eds, *Sport and Leisure in Contemporary Society* (London, Polytechnic of Central London, 1975).
14   M. Kaplan, *Leisure in America* (New York, Wiley, 1960), p. 62.
15   K. K. Sillitoe, *Planning for Leisure* (London, HMSO, 1969), p. 17.
16   N. C. A. Parry and D. Johnson, *Leisure in Hatfield, Stage II*, Dept of Psychological and Social Studies, Hatfield Polytechnic, August 1973.
17   E. T. Ashton, *People and Leisure* (London, Ginn, 1971), p. 48.
18   Roberts, *op. cit.*, p. 46. See also S. Parker, 'Professional Life and Leisure', *New Society*, 10 October 1974.
19   W. E. Thompson and G. F. Streib, 'Meaningful Activity in a Family Context', in R. W. Kleemeier, ed., *Aging and Leisure* (New York, Oxford University Press, 1961), p. 184.
20   Roberts, *op. cit.*, pp. 47–8.
21   Ashton, *op. cit.*, p. 57.
22   E. Shanas *et al.*, *Old People in Three Industrial Societies* (New York, Atherton Press, 1968), p. 292.
23   A. Harris and S. Parker, 'Leisure and the Elderly', in Smith *et al.*, eds, *op. cit.*
24   C. K. Brightbill, *The Challenge of Leisure* (Englewood Cliffs, Prentice-Hall, 1960), p. 73.
25   C. R. W. Smith, 'Leisure Activities of Impaired Persons', in A. Harris, *Handicapped and Impaired in Great Britain* (London, HMSO, 1971), p. 93.
26   O. von Mering and F. L. Weniger, 'Social-Cultural Background of the Ageing Individual', in J. E. Birren, ed., *Handbook of Ageing and the Individual* (University of Chicago Press, 1959), p. 321.
27   Sillitoe, *op. cit.*, p. 174.
28   Harris and Parker, *op. cit.*, p. 175.
29   Ashton, *op. cit.*, p. 64.
30   E. Cumming and W. E. Henry, *Growing Old* (New York, Basic Books, 1961), p. 14.
31   J. Tunstall, *Old and Alone* (London, Routledge, 1966), p. 240.
32   G. F. Streib and C. J. Schneider, *Retirement in American Society* (Ithaca, Cornell University Press, 1971), p. 182.
33   M. P. Crawford, 'Retirement and Role-Playing', *Sociology*, May 1972.
34   R. Rapoport *et al.*, *Leisure and the Family Life Cycle* (London, Routledge, 1975).

PART TWO LEISURE AND OTHER SPHERES OF LIFE

Chapter 5

Leisure and Work

In many ways leisure is bound up with work. It is easy to think of leisure as the *opposite* of work, or to define it as time left over after work. But the relationship between these two spheres of life goes much deeper than that. Not all human societies have made the same distinction between leisure and work that most of us make in the modern industrial world. As compared with other times in history and other parts of the world, leisure and work today show certain broad features and trends. Work influences leisure in many ways and some observers believe the opposite influence is becoming more apparent. We shall take a look at the various theories which have recently been developed to explain the different possible types of relationship between work and leisure. Then we shall consider how far it is valid to regard 'creative' leisure as an answer to some of the problems of 'uncreative' work.

Leisure and work in other societies

Life in primitive societies follows a pre-determined pattern in which work and non-work are inextricably confused. Rosalie Wax remarks on this fusion of leisure and work: 'I do not believe that any Bushman could tell us – or would be interested in telling us – which part of [his] activity was work and which was play.'[1] The rural life has always involved an integration of leisure and work in such a way that the one is continuous with the other rather than separate from it. The tradition of the artist and the craftsman, too, is one in which there is no split between work and play. In the words of C. Wright Mills, the simple self-expression of play and the creation of the ulterior

E

value of work are combined in work-as-craftsmanship.[2] The artist is at work and at play in the same act.

But another set of traditions *have* made a distinction between work and leisure, and it is arguable that such a distinction, and the values which support it, have played a central part in the development of industrial civilisation. As we saw in Chapter 1, the ancient Greeks insisted that work could have nothing to do with leisure. To them, work was a necessary material evil, which the leisurely elite should avoid.[3] Various religious views of work have, through the ages, stressed its importance as a means of individual salvation and service to others (in Chapter 8 we shall discuss these in more detail). If leisure fits into this scheme of things at all, it is only as re-creation, restoring man for the next day of work.

Leisure and work today

In modern society we find three broad approaches to leisure and work. One (which is clearly declining) is in the religious tradition mentioned above: work perceived as the serious business of life and leisure as subsidiary or even non-existent. The second approach represents a complete swing of the pendulum: leisure seen as the aim of life, and work as merely a means to that end. Thirdly, we have the beginnings of a more integrated approach to both leisure and work, appreciating them as reconcilable parts of a whole, each able to enrich the other, rather like the life of the craftsman or artist.

Thus in terms of the ways in which individuals perceive the relationship between work and leisure in their own lives we may distinguish three patterns: (1) priority of work, (2) priority of leisure, and (3) equality of work and leisure. One way of finding out how many people, and what kinds of people, have each of these patterns is to ask them questions about their 'central life interest'. This is a term coined by Robert Dubin to refer to a significant area of social experience.[4] Assuming that participation in a sphere may be necessary but not important to an individual, he classified replies to a series of three-choice questions as job-oriented, non-job-oriented, or indifferent. By a margin of three to one, work was found to be not a central life interest for industrial workers. However, Louis Orzack gave an amended version of Dubin's schedule to a sample of professional nurses, and confirmed the hypothesis that work *would* be a central life interest to them.[5]

These and other studies suggest that people will identify more strongly with either work or non-work, depending to a large extent on how fulfilling their work is. People who say that work is the most important, interesting, etc. thing in their lives are not necessarily saying that their lives are devoid of leisure-like experiences. Perhaps they are able to get from work some of the satisfactions which other people get from leisure. Also, there may be cultural influences operating which produce a change in people's attitudes over quite a short space of time. A Japanese study in 1967 showed that more than half the people polled gave priority to work and a third gave equal priority to work and leisure. A similar study in 1971 showed that the 'equal priority' view was then held by 89 per cent.[6] We may conclude that both type of work and type of culture affect the relative importance accorded to leisure in the life pattern.

Another clue to the relative importance attached to work and leisure is the choice that people make between having more income or more leisure. Given the separation between work and leisure which requires one to work 'for a living', the question arises of how much one should work so as to have both time and money for leisure. Some economists argue that, after people receive a comfortable margin over what they consider to be necessary, they will not seek additional work.[7] This is no doubt true of most simpler, non-industrial societies, but the evidence is that among the economically advanced nations of the world more people prefer additional work or a second job to more leisure. In 1969 two out of five 'moonlighters' in the United States claimed a need for additional income for *regular* household expenses.[8] There may come a time when most people will choose more leisure instead of more income, but that time does not seem imminent.

The influence of work on leisure

Experience in, and attitudes to, work influence leisure in a number of ways. The scheduling of the work will determine how much time is available for leisure, and the content of the work may affect the amount and type of energies left over for leisure. Cultural differences enable the same kind of work to affect leisure variously from country to country. Some jobs will permit 'leisure at work' more than others, and some occupations are more frequently associated with certain kinds of leisure activities than others. We summarise below some of the main research findings relevant to all these issues.

Child and Macmillan have taken a comparative look at the leisure lives of managers in Britain, the United States and other countries.[9] Results from several surveys suggest that many American managers are completely job-oriented, intellectually narrow, and uninterested in the humanities or liberal arts. The evidence is that the typical American executive enjoys his work, and that his way of life permits no clear-cut distinction between work and leisure. The picture emerging from surveys of British managers, however, is quite different. Work-related activities do not take up a major part of their leisure time. They generally spend most of their leisure time at home, and few devote any appreciable part of it to activities that in any way directly further their work and career.

Several studies throw light on aspects of the work and leisure lives of manual workers. Richard Brown and his colleagues show that, while home- and family-based activities predominate in the leisure of shipbuilding workers, some of their leisure activities take place in work time.[10] Very often the social meeting places at work are more fixed and permanent than the places in the yard where the work is actually done, and shipyard workers talk about their 'leisure-at-work'. James Mott traces the historical association between miners and weavers and pigeon racing and breeding.[11] Drawing on research carried out by French sociologists in a mining area, he suggests that the complex business of pigeon racing provides individual and social compensations, and the opportunity to exercise many kinds of skill lacking in mine work. Jeremy Tunstall describes a different kind of compensatory leisure behaviour indulged in by some distant-water fishermen: the hard drinking, 'living it up' and status-seeking activities of people who are ashore for only three months in the year.[12]

Some types of worker tend to carry work attitudes over into the weekend in spite of fatigue and often an expressed desire to get away from work and everything it stands for. Fred Blum discusses the relation between work and leisure experienced by the typical packing-house worker.[13] Since it is almost impossible to work eight hours intensively and switch over suddenly to a new, creative way of life, these workers are pushed into some kind of activity which keeps them occupied without reminding them of their work. Fishing is one of their favourite pastimes. It has some elements which are just the opposite of work – relaxing outdoors 'away from it all' – yet it is in other ways continuous with work and requires no basic change of attitude. Also, the *style* of a particular leisure activity may be related to work experience. Thus K. Etzkorn notes that 'public campground' camping, which is routinised, is practised more by individuals with routinised jobs, while 'wilderness' camping is preferred by individuals in more creative jobs.[14]

Several American studies have sought to establish a relationship between type of occupation and choice of leisure activity. Leonard Reissman found that people in higher class positions were more active and diverse in their social and leisure participation than those in lower classes.[15] Saxon Graham concluded that the proportion of professional workers participating in strenuous exercise was nearly twice that of unskilled workers.[16] Sometimes occupational 'prestige' is taken to be the variable, as with the studies of Alfred Clarke[17] and Rabel Burdge.[18] The general conclusion is that people in the higher prestige classes participate in a greater variety of leisure activities than do people in the lower classes, although a few pursuits, such as bowling and gardening, are more favoured by the lower classes. But one wonders whether the fairly gross categories of 'prestige level 1', etc. conceal more specific differences in occupations which may be linked with characteristic forms of leisure behaviour.

In an article titled 'The Long Arm of the Job', Martin Meissner poses the question: does work affect leisure?[19] He is particularly interested in three dimensions of both work and leisure: the amount of choice or discretion that is possible or demanded, the extent to which the activity is purpose-directed or carried out for its own sake (instrumental or expressive), and the amount of social interaction involved. He concludes that when choice of action is suppressed by the constraints of the work process, the worker's capacity for meeting the demands of spare-time activities which require discretion is reduced: he engages less in those activities which necessitate planning, coordination and purposeful action, but more in sociable and expressive activities. Lack of opportunity to talk on the job is associated with much reduced rates of participation in associations, that is, in activity commonly believed to help integrate individuals into the community.

The examples of work influences on leisure considered so far have been British or American, but the cross-cultural nature of these influences is illustrated by Ezra Vogel's study of middle-class Japan.[20] The Japanese businessman, like the American, finds it difficult to distinguish working time from leisure time, and often entertains his clients with a trip to the golf course or a party with entertainment with geisha girls. Like successful businessmen, doctors rarely make a sharp separation between work and leisure, partly because to some extent working hours are determined by the arrival of patients. It is the salaried man who makes the sharpest distinction between working time and free time. He generally has set hours so that he can plan certain hours of the day and certain days of the week for himself and his family.

All the above studies are reports on static situations. What happens to leisure when work routines change? Rolf Meyersohn describes the consequences for leisure of an American aircraft factory giving its employees a three-day weekend every month without a reduction in total weekly hours worked.[21] At first the general attitude to the change was favourable, but after a while more people became dissatisfied with the three-day weekend and fewer made definite plans about how to spend such future weekends. The findings of that particular survey may be biased because it took place at a time of economic recession. Edwin Blakelock examined the effect of rotating shift work on leisure activities, and concluded that such workers were generally less active in their leisure and tended to spend more time around the house than did other workers.[22] This was mainly because they had less of their leisure time when most people were having theirs.

The regular four-day week is a development which has much potential for affecting leisure. Riva Poor wrote a book on this in 1970, at which time she had located in the United States 'three dozen 4-day firms and over 7,000 4-day employees – and a few 3-day firms as well'.[23] In a later edition of the book she claimed that by 1972 over 4,000 articles had been written on the subject – but there was nothing to suggest that more than a tiny fraction of employees were at that time on a four-day week. Research quoted by Riva Poor suggests that, while some workers like the bunching of free time which is more useful for old and new leisure activities, others complain that the longer working day is fatiguing. A rearrangement of the same number of working hours is probably not so important for leisure as an absolute reduction in working hours.

There are arguments for and against the proposition that work and leisure are becoming similar to each other. This is sometimes known as the 'fusion' versus 'polarity' debate.[24] Part of the arguments for fusion are relevant here: the ways in which leisure is said to be becoming more like work. More people are using leisure for work purposes – to advance their careers, like the managers quoted earlier in this chapter, or as part of the work task, like 'customers' golf' for sales executives. Gregory Stone perceives an attitude change: 'more and more we work at our play . . . we begin to evaluate our leisure in terms of the potential it has for work – for us to "do it ourselves" '.[25] The popular game of bingo has several features which are similar to the work experience of many of those who take part in it: it involves concentration and regulated patterns of physical movement, is supervised by someone else, and allows breaks for refreshments. Ski school is another example: for beginners to keep up with the exacting requirements of the instructor can be an exhausting experience. Indeed, many sporting and artistic activities have more in common with physically and mentally demanding work than with the idle and carefree attitude that is often thought to be the essence of leisure.

The influence of leisure on work

The other half of the 'fusion' argument is the attempt to demonstrate how work is becoming more like leisure. Many devices are being invented for creating spaces of free time within the working day and at intervals throughout the career. Although no solid data are available, it is probable that the 'coffee break' is today more frequent, and the average lunch 'hour' longer, than previously. The sabbatical year is no longer exclusive to academic employees. One American firm has for some time been granting twelve months' paid holiday after ten years of service, and other employees have the chance of a quarter-sabbatical – three months off after five years' service. Another type of work–leisure fusion, the integration of sex into work, is noted by Herbert Marcuse: 'Without ceasing to be an instrument of labor, the body is allowed to exhibit its sexual features in the everyday work world and in work relations.'[26]

The above changes are perhaps not of great significance in themselves, but collectively they may be seen to indicate a broad trend in modern society away from work and toward leisure. They link up with the claim that we are in process of developing a 'society of leisure'.

Dumazedier has assembled a number of findings from his study in France to support his contention that the effects of leisure on work are now more marked than vice versa.[27] Many young people are looking for the leisure possibilities in any job they are choosing. Executives and their wives are refusing to accept a local situation where afterwork life is underdeveloped. Company organisation itself is often based upon methods of emulation, cooperation and competition borrowed from sports, and numerous methods of job improvement and training have been inspired by techniques well known to sports instructors. While Dumazedier appears to favour most of these developments, he also draws attention to the negative side of the picture: enjoyment of recreational activities often results in denial of any commitment to either company or union. It should also be noted that his general approach to work and leisure is based on an assessment of trends in France: the situation in Britain, with a different balance between industrial and agricultural activities, may lead to different conclusions.

The influence of leisure on work is also seen in the fact that a substantial and growing proportion of the population is employed in one or other of the leisure industries. These include industries providing entertainment, sports and gambling facilities, holiday amenities, materials for hobbies, a considerable part of transport, book production, the care of gardens and pets, and so on. Employees in these occupations often face the paradox that other people's leisure is their own work. As compared with most 'ordinary' occupations, those in the leisure industries tend to allow considerable scope for 'role style' or personalised performance, authority and sanctions when rules are broken are likely to be asserted only when the public are not present, and there are special strains and tensions resulting from playing a role – waitress or comedian, for example – which must closely match the expectations of the paying customers.

Types of work–leisure relationship

Earlier in this chapter mention was made of the 'fusion' or 'polarity' of work and leisure in respect of social developments in these two spheres. But what of work and leisure as parts of each of our lives? We may speak of fusion if we refuse to divide our lives in this way, and we may speak of polarity if we insist on such a division. The corresponding functions of leisure have been labelled by Harold Wilensky as 'spillover' and 'compensatory'.[28] Work may be said to spill over into leisure to the extent that leisure is the continuation of work experiences and attitudes; leisure is compensatory if it seeks to make up for dissatisfactions felt in work.

My own research has involved carrying the analysis of these two types of relationship further, and led to the addition of a third.[29] I distinguish extension, opposition and neutrality. With the *extension* pattern the similarity of at least some work and leisure activities and the lack of demarcation between work and leisure are the key characteristics. This pattern is typically shown by social workers, successful businessmen (perhaps they *are* successful because they have little or no time for leisure), doctors, teachers, and similar people. The key aspects of the *opposition* pattern are the intentional dissimilarity of work and leisure and the strong demarcation between the two spheres. People with tough physical jobs like miners and oil-rig workers may either hate their work so much that any reminder of it in their off-duty time is unpleasant, or they may have a love-hate attitude to it. A third pattern of *neutrality* is only partly defined by a 'usually different' content of work and leisure and an 'average' demarcation of spheres. It is *not* intermediate between the other two patterns because it denotes detachment from work rather than either positive or negative attachment. It often goes along with jobs which Peter Berger called 'gray' – neither fulfilling nor oppressive.[30] Such people tend to be as passive and uninvolved in their leisure as they are in their work.

My own and other research suggests that each of the three patterns of work–leisure relationship is associated with a number of other work and non-work variables. People with high autonomy in their work are likely to have the extension pattern, and those with low autonomy the neutrality pattern (the effect of autonomy on the opposition pattern is not clear). Extension is usually accompanied by a feeling of being 'stretched' by the work, neutrality by being 'bored' with it, and opposition by being 'damaged' by it. The likelihood of having some work colleagues among one's close friends seems to be high among those with the extension pattern and low among the neutrality group. Level of education usually goes from high to low among the groups with the extension, neutrality and opposition patterns.

These and other conclusions about the three patterns are tentative and remain to be verified or modified by subsequent research.[31] As critics have pointed out, the three-fold typology leaves many questions open.[32] People do not necessarily find either the work or the leisure they want; so their needs and wishes cannot necessarily be assessed from their behaviour in a given situation. There may be more people seeking 'extension' or 'compensation' than actually finding it. Also, the existence of patterns of 'extension', 'opposition' and 'neutrality' between people's work and leisure is no guarantee that there is any causal relationship between experiences in the two areas of life.

Kenneth Roberts has suggested that it is important to distinguish ideas from behaviour, because relationships discovered between work and leisure on the ideational plane will not necessarily be reflected in behaviour.[33] Leisure could be more potent than work in giving meaning to an individual's life, yet it could be his job that influenced his leisure behaviour more than vice versa. Roberts notes that the division between individual and societal levels of analysis cuts across the distinction between behavioural and ideational planes. Leisure has, he claims, advanced most in the individual–behavioural and ideational–societal spheres, reflecting respectively more time freed from work and the marketing of leisure values by the relevant industries. In the individual–ideational and behavioural–societal spheres, however, work values and socially-structured behaviour still indicate a rhythm of life dictated by the demands of work.

Another approach to work–leisure relationships is found in the functional tradition of sociological theory. Briefly, this theory, whose foremost exponent is Talcott Parsons, is concerned with the types of problem which have to be solved for society to survive and evolve. These problems, and the sub-systems of society which face them, are adaptation (the economy), goal attainment (the political system), integration (family or ethnic groups), and latency (the cultural system). Edward Gross has applied this theory to leisure and work.[34] He points to the *adaptation* functions of recreation and creative leisure in compensating for the fatiguing or deadening effect of some forms of work; the *goal attainment* functions which are served by assigning differential access to leisure opportunities; the *integration* functions of sociability and horsing around at work; and the *latency* functions of colleague groups of 'mutually trusting equals who drink coffee or play cards together'. This theory may be criticised as a somewhat strained attempt to put leisure behaviour into four boxes, and it is questionable whether it adds very much to our understanding of the relationship between leisure and work.

Two fairly recent theoretical articles have aimed at clarifying and simplifying the various concepts and theories which have grown up. Kando and Summers draw attention to the need to integrate the study of *forms* of work and leisure and their underlying significance or *meaning*.[35] Similar forms of work or non-work may have different meanings for various individuals participating in them, and different forms may have similar underlying meanings. The authors' model attempts to conceive the complex set of relationships within which work influences non-work. It suggests two paths: (1) work leads to the development of certain psychological, social, and behavioural skills and life-styles which may spill over into leisure, and (2) work, when it leads to a certain subjective experience of deprivation, may result in efforts to compensate for this in non-work activity.

John Kelly is also concerned with the problem of meaning, but he thinks that asking why participants engage in an activity is a dubious procedure, since all of us construct 'reasons' to fit situational expectations and self-images.[36] He prefers reports by self and others of behaviour and activity. He believes that work–leisure relation and discretion are the two most important dimensions. Leisure may be either independent of work or dependent on the meaning given it by work. It may also be either freely chosen or determined by work constraints or the pervasive norms of the society. This analysis gives four cells: (1) chosen and independent: 'pure' leisure, as in the Greek ideal; (2) chosen but related to work: 'spillover' leisure; (3) determined by the structural or social factors of work but independent of the work relation: 'complementary' leisure; and (4) determined by and related to work: 'preparation' or 'recuperation' leisure.

The above sketches are intended to give an idea of the range of theories which have been put forward in recent years to explain the relationship between work and leisure. Most researchers agree that there is a long way to go, both in terms of empirical enquiry and in the construction of theory, before we can feel confident that we 'understand' this complex process. The subject is of wide concern, and relevant findings bear not only upon the way we attempt to influence and control social behaviour and institutions but also upon the way in which we handle work and leisure problems and make choices in our own lives.

The 'leisure solution' to work

Some people take an approach to leisure which amounts to seeing it, not as a sphere of life in its own right, but as something which can help to solve various problems connected with work. Whether on the one hand we 'fuse' and spill over work into leisure, or on the other hand 'polarise' the two or use one as compensation for the other, depends to a large extent on how far we think we can divide up our lives and the parts of our society into separate compartments. There is the further point that, having divided our lives or our society to a certain degree, we can ask ourselves whether we *like* the result – whether we want to continue the process of division, or try to reverse the trend by aiming at greater unity.

Sociologists and psychologists who have studied the ways in which most people experience their work today, whether white-collar or blue-collar, generally conclude that there are fewer opportunities than in the past for feelings of self-expression and creativity in work. As an answer to this, some critics want to tackle the content, organisation and environment of the work itself. More relevant to the focus of our concern in this work are the ideas of those who want to use leisure as compensation for work. As Wilensky puts it, they want to 'develop patterns of creative, challenging leisure to compensate for an inevitable spread in dehumanized labor'.[37]

Leaving aside the question of whether the spread of 'dehumanized labor' *is* inevitable, we can take note of what research scholars have concluded about the compensation idea. The evidence they have gathered does not, in general, support it. In consequence of his study of alienation in various forms of work, Robert Blauner concluded that the problem with the leisure solution is that it underestimates the fact that work remains the single most important activity for most people in terms of time and energy.[38] The leisure solution ignores the subtle ways in which the quality of one's work life affects the quality of one's leisure. Furthermore, the implicit policy of emphasising leisure as a solution to the problems of unfree work would involve a basic inequality – a division of society into one section of consumers who are creative in their leisure time but have meaningless work, and a second segment capable of self-realisation in both spheres of life.

The organisation theorist Chris Argyris has reviewed a number of studies of work and leisure from the standpoint of personality and organisation theory.[39] He is critical of the idea that leisure can be used as compensation for work and that there is a kind of trade-off between the two spheres. The model of man used in personality and organisation theory would require that the compensation theory be rejected. The logic is as follows. If individuals tend to experience dependence, submission, frustration, conflict, and short time perspective at work, and if they adapt to these conditions by psychological withdrawal, apathy, indifference, and a decrease in the importance of their worth as human beings, these adaptive activities become more important in the person's life and they will guide his leisure behaviour outside the workplace. Individuals will seek leisure activities that are consonant with the adaptive activities. To take one example, it was found that when play was encouraged on the job the employee became more committed to his job, more energetic in his leisure, and a more effective contributor to society in his political activity and ideology.

Another relevant study is that of Bishop and Ikeda, who examined thirty-two leisure activities of people in eighteen occupations.[40] They concluded that the active leisure of those in high-prestige occupations might indicate a compensatory leisure mechanism for the sedentary life in many such occupations. But people in more masculine occupations tended to participate in masculine-oriented leisure, while those in feminine occupations tended to choose feminine-oriented leisure. Beyond these two patterns, the researchers suggested a third: work and leisure may be contrasted in terms of their energy requirements but similar in terms of their sociability requirements. In other words, compensation may be a more physical process, and spillover a more mental process.

With rapid changes taking place in our society affecting both work and leisure, we need to consider which path to take in the future to help guide events in the direction we would like. Denis Johnston has suggested that there are three probable alternative scenarios.[41] The first is of an automated society in which a small number of people would be responsible for production and distribution of goods, with the remainder of the population limited to consumption. The corresponding ethic would be a takeover by leisure of the intrinsic and personally satisfying aspects of life, with work being accepted primarily for the monetary rewards it brings. The second scenario recognises the realisation and maintenance of a full-employment economy, and assumes the maintenance of the work ethic, with a steady flow of appropriately trained persons willing to work. The third scenario suggests a gradual reunification of work and leisure into a holistic pattern characteristic of most pre-industrial societies. The economic sector would be linked more closely to non-economic forces, so that non-material cultural values would tend to become the primary determinants of what we produce and consume.

This last scenario would be consistent with the belief that the sphere of leisure could be as productive and worthwhile as that of creative work, entailing the same sort of personal commitment and providing the same sort of satisfaction and fulfilment. This conception of leisure would be opposed to the idea of 'job' or externally-constrained work time, but not opposed to the idea of having a *work* to do.[42]

REFERENCES

1 R. H. Wax, 'Free Time in Other Cultures', in W. Donahue et al., eds, *Free Time: Challenge to Later Maturity* (Ann Arbor, University of Michigan Press, 1958), p. 4.

2 C. W. Mills, *White Collar* (New York, Oxford University Press, 1956), p. 222.

3 A. Tilgher, *Work: What It Has Meant to Men through the Ages* (London, Harrap, 1931). Also summarised in C. W. Mills, *op. cit.*, pp. 215–18.

4 R. Dubin, 'Industrial Workers' Worlds', *Social Problems*, January 1956.

5 L. Orzack, 'Work as a "Central Life Interest" of Professionals', *Social Problems*, Autumn 1959.

6 'Fuji Bank Bulletin', July 1972.

7 P. Samuelson, *Economics* (New York, McGraw-Hill), 1967, p. 549.

8 G. H. Moore and J. N. Hedges, 'Trends in Labor and Leisure', *Monthly Labor Review*, February 1971.

9 J. Child and B. Macmillan, 'Managers and their Leisure', in M. A. Smith et al., eds, *Leisure and Society in Britain* (London, Allen Lane, 1973).

10 R. Brown et al., 'Leisure in Work: The "Occupational Culture" of Ship-building Workers', in Smith et al., eds, *op. cit.*

11 J. Mott, 'Miners, Weavers and Pigeon Racing', in Smith et al., eds, *op. cit.*

12 J. Tunstall, *The Fishermen* (London, MacGibbon & Kee), 1962.

13 F. H. Blum, *Toward a Democratic Work Process* (New York, Harper, 1953), pp. 109–10.

14 K. P. Etzkorn, 'Leisure and Camping: The Social Meaning of a Form of Public Recreation', *Sociology and Social Research*, October 1964.

15 L. Reissman, 'Class, Leisure and Social Participation', *American Sociological Review*, February 1954.

16 S. Graham, 'Social Correlates of Adult Leisure-Time Behaviour', in M. B. Sussman, ed., *Community Structure and Analysis* (New York, Crowell, 1959), p. 347.

17 A. C. Clarke, 'The Use of Leisure and its Relation to Levels of Occupational Prestige', *American Sociological Review*, June 1956.

18 R. J. Burdge, 'Levels of Occupational Prestige and Leisure Activity', *Journal of Leisure Research*, Summer 1969.

19 M. Meissner, 'The Long Arm of the Job', *Industrial Relations*, October 1971.

20 E. F. Vogel, *Japan's New Middle Class* (Berkeley, University of California Press, 1963), p. 21.

21 R. Meyersohn, 'Changing Work and Leisure Routines', in E. O. Smigel, ed., *Work and Leisure* (New Haven, College and University Press), 1963.

22 E. H. Blakelock, 'A Durkheimian Approach to Some Temporal Problems of Leisure', *Social Problems*, Summer 1961.

23 R. Poor, *4 Days, 40 Hours* (Cambridge, Mass., Bursk & Poor, 1970).

24 D. Riesman and W. Blomberg, 'Work and Leisure: Fusion or Polarity?', in C. M. Arensberg et al., eds, *Research in Industrial Human Relations* (New York, Harper, 1957), p. 93.

25 G. P. Stone, 'American Sports: Play and Display', in E. Larrabee and R. Meyersohn, eds, *Mass Leisure* (Glencoe, Free Press, 1958), p. 285.

26 H. Marcuse, *One-Dimensional Man* (London, Routledge, 1964), p. 74.

27 J. Dumazedier, *Toward a Society of Leisure* (New York, Collier-Macmillan, 1967), p. 75.

28   H. Wilensky, 'Work, Careers and Social Integration', *International Social Science Journal*, No. 4, 1960.

29   S. R. Parker, *The Future of Work and Leisure* (London, Paladin, 1972), Chapter 8.

30   P. Berger, *The Human Shape of Work* (New York, Macmillan, 1964), pp. 218–19.

31   For example, R. Lansbury, 'Careers, Work and Leisure Among the New Professionals', *Sociological Review*, August 1974.

32   A. Clayre, *Work and Play* (London, Weidenfeld & Nicolson, 1974), p. 198.

33   K. Roberts, 'The Changing Relationship Between Work and Leisure', in I. Appleton, ed., *Leisure Research and Policy* (Edinburgh, Scottish Academic Press, 1974).

34   E. Gross, 'A Functional Approach to Leisure Analysis', *Social Problems*, Summer 1961.

35   T. M. Kando and W. C. Summers, 'The Impact of Work on Leisure', *Pacific Sociological Review*, July 1971.

36   J. R. Kelly, 'Work and Leisure: A Simplified Paradigm', *Journal of Leisure Research*, Winter 1972.

37   Wilensky, *op. cit.*, p. 546.

38   R. Blauner, *Alienation and Freedom* (Chicago, University Press, 1964), p. 183.

39   C. Argyris, 'Personality and Organization Theory Revisited', *Administrative Science Quarterly*, June 1973.

40   D. W. Bishop and M. Ikeda, 'Status and Role Factors in the Leisure Behaviour of Different Occupations', *Sociology and Social Research*, no. 2, 1970.

41   D. F. Johnston, 'The Future of Work: Three Possible Alternatives', *Monthly Labor Review*, May 1972.

42   T. F. Green, *Work, Leisure and the American Schools* (New York, Random House, 1968), p. 92.

Chapter 6

Leisure and the Family

The extent to which leisure has been spent within the circle of the family has changed during the course of history. Today the family is still a primary source of the developing leisure attitudes of its young members, although other influences compete with those of the family in shaping leisure behaviour. Despite the growth of commercialised leisure, there are still many forms of recreation which family members enjoy together, though adolescents are often an exception to this. There are differences between the various social classes in respect of the part played by the family in the leisure activities of its members and in the degree to which leisure is spent in the home. We shall examine the ways in which men and women have different leisure roles in the contemporary family structure and as individuals.

The history of family recreation

Until comparatively recently in the history of mankind, there was no such thing as family recreation. In the past, what little leisure men and women had was spent chiefly in the company of their own sex.[1] If a man desired female companionship, he could hardly obtain it from his wife, since she lived in a different world. Most societies were male-dominated, and women were too submissive to achieve the equality which companionship requires. To fill this need of the more privileged men, special women were often available (such as the *heterae* of ancient Greece and the *geisha* of Japan), unmarried women, trained to please men with their intellectual, aesthetic or sexual skills.

In the more recent past, a century or more ago, the family unit had developed its maximum functions, which included providing for a large part of the recreational life of its members. In very small communities, the play of children and adults occurred in or around family dwellings, since these were often the only buildings.[2] Among the occupants of country houses and village cottages, much recreation consisted of family visiting, particularly on a Sunday, though travel itself was not considered recreation because of its discomforts.

It must not be thought, however, that the nineteenth century represents a golden age during which family leisure reached a peak from which there has been a subsequent decline. Rather, what has happened is that a great variety of relatively new leisure activities have been *added* to the experience of most families. Indeed, Ronald Fletcher argues against the proposition that there has been a diminution of family functions in relation to leisure, and he maintains that, even in pre-industrial Britain, recreative activities seem to have involved groups going beyond the family.[3] Clark Vincent agrees with this analysis when applied to American society. He remarks that it is quite possible that today's family produces more of its own recreation than did the family of fifty or a hundred years ago.[4] The family function of 'consuming' recreation is today greater than ever – one has only to think of the millions of pounds spent annually on home sports, games, cameras, camping, and many other family pursuits.

The family as a source of leisure attitudes

The family – society's primary agent of socialisation – provides a setting in which the attitudes of children are developed towards all major institutions, including recreation and leisure. Within the family 'good' and 'bad' ways of behaving are learned: when and how to play, with whom, what to do and what not to do. Some parents have a 'serious' approach toward leisure pursuits which they try to pass on to their children. Max Kaplan cites music lessons as an example: some parents arrange these for their children because music is 'good' and will give pleasure in the future.[5] But many children do not react well to concentrated application to arts such as music, and so the private tutoring system in the home ('taking lessons') has given way to the pleasanter social experience of the school class period.

The influence of parents on the development of their children's attitudes to leisure should not, however, be overstated. If we accept the theme of 'youth culture' (see Chapter 4), we shall recognise the extent to which older children live more and more in a society of their own, and find the family a less and less satisfying psychological home.[6] One of the main reasons for this is the relative instability of the modern family, which is likely to be geographically mobile and to have a high risk of the parents divorcing, with consequent disruption for the children. This applies to the families of the middle class and of the 'new' working class, though it is less true of the traditional working class. In these circumstances there may be a lack of meaningful contact between parents and children during leisure hours. To remedy this situation, those who are concerned with the personality development of children advocate a close and continuous contact between parents and their children, and they see family recreation activities as one way of helping to build and maintain this contact.[7]

It is possible to show that the typical family relationships and attitudes in a culture have a profound effect on the function and meaning of particular leisure activities for its members. Zurcher and Meadow have discussed the way in which alternative types of socialisation process in different types of culture lead to correspondingly different national sports.[8] In Mexican culture the family is male-dominated and severely authoritarian. Young boys typically react to the tyranny of their fathers by attempting to dominate their younger siblings, while wives and daughters react by forming a 'female mutual protection society'. The bullfight, Zurcher and Meadow suggest, re-lives aspects of this frustration-producing family situation, and provides an outlet for socially acceptable aggression. The bull is symbolic of the father and the matador of the son. In watching the matador defeat the bull, the Mexican male is said to be able to compensate symbolically for deprivations suffered at the hands of his tyrannical father, while women spectators are able to express their generalised hostility to men – including perhaps an unconscious desire for the matador to be killed as well as the bull.

By contrast, in the typical American family the byword is equality, and authority tends to be muted. Parents are expected to be the 'buddies' of their children but at the same time to socialise them into the dominant values of society. This still requires authority, and leads to some frustration and aggression in the children, whose problem becomes: how can one overtly show hostility to a 'buddy'? Hostility is consequently rationalised and disguised with verbal repartee – a pattern which is reflected in the American national sport. Baseball is a highly elaborate game in which equality is a central ethic. It mutes aggression behind its reciprocity, rules, records and rituals. It may be said to duplicate the vagueness and intellectual nature of conflict in the American family and to provide a controlled means of expressing hostility toward authority.

Family leisure activities

The home is the place where family members do most of their television viewing, reading, indulging in hobbies and general relaxing. Most social contact with relatives and friends occurs in the context of the home. Although it would be an exaggeration to say that the spending of leisure at home is new, it has certainly grown in comparison with the past. Formerly the man of the house went to the corner store, the barber shop, the 'pub', the *Gasthaus* or café; the children came into the house only to eat and sleep, while the mother took her chair out to sit with other women on the pavement.[9] Today the average home has become a more inviting place in which to spend leisure time. The higher material standard of living has enabled improvements to be made in the size, appearance and furnishing of many (though by no means all) homes. The home furnishing industries with their high-pressure advertising and the home-beautiful magazines have played their part in this process, which has also been helped by relevant school courses and other educational efforts.

Kaplan has raised the interesting question of how far sociability is a form of leisure and what forms it takes in family life. He sees sociability as a quality of relationship, essentially a liking for people and their company.[10] Although it is strictly speaking only the mother and father who have 'chosen' each other as personalities, the rest of the family group are likely to seek a quality of life together based on pleasurable interaction. This does not necessarily mean extended or frequent conversation between family members. In a situation in which each person values the presence of others (or at least their being 'around'), symbolic communication may be more important than conversation: little things, gestures, small motions become clearer as there is closer rapport. As Kaplan points out, there are no statistics to show that couples who divorce have talked less to each other than other couples. Perhaps they talked more, and intensely!

Allied to sociability is the question of the contribution leisure can make to family cohesiveness. According to Carlson, recreation can either weaken or strengthen family ties.[11] Parents busy with activities away from home are often only too glad to let the children go their separate ways and are grateful to organisations that will fill the children's leisure hours. However, recreation can and should serve to strengthen a family and keep it together; it is possible through leisure-time pursuits to maintain family solidarity and unity of purpose. Through recreation children may learn the lessons in responsibility and consideration for other members of the family once learned through home chores. Support for the proposition that family cohesiveness is influenced by outdoor recreation comes from West and Merriam.[12] As a measure of cohesiveness they used the amount of intimate communication of troubles, secrets and mood among family members. They found that outdoor recreation helps maintain and increase family cohesiveness, especially for those in the earlier stages of the life-cycle.

At all stages of the life-cycle – except for adolescents and those who do not marry – a substantial proportion of leisure activities are likely to take place within the family circle. Adolescents usually share little of the home-centred family life of their parents.[13] They generally contribute little to the do-it-yourself activities of home improvement.

They do not travel with their parents in the family car, although they may occasionally borrow it if they have none of their own. They are much less likely than in the past to take their holidays with their parents. They go out more often than other age groups to places of entertainment, but usually with members of their peer-group. For parents and young children, however, the family circle is likely to be a primary centre for their leisure activities.

A national survey revealed that the car and television are the two biggest influences on leisure behaviour in Britain.[14] The researchers pointed out that these influences are opposed, in the sense that one keeps people out of doors while the other keeps them indoors. Both, however, may keep members of the family together and help to strengthen the family as a unit. An examination of leisure activities carried out with other members of the family showed that 59 per cent of the individuals in the survey who went camping did so as part of a family group. Swimming and hiking also seemed often to be a family matter, as were tennis and fishing to a lesser extent. This particular research project was concerned mainly with outdoor activity, and it is obvious that many indoor pursuits, such as playing cards or other games, also involve the family.

Since its proliferation in the 1950s, television has dominated the leisure hours of the mass of people. Its effect on family life and leisure remains to some extent controversial, and we need to distinguish different periods in the growth of television viewing. Until the period of the immediate post-war years, active participant recreation and passive entertainment outside the home had been steadily gaining ground, resulting in a diminishing amount of leisure time being spent within the family circle. For a while, during the 1950s, it looked as though television would bring the family together again in front of the single receiver in the living-room.[15] One early assessment was that television 'has a tendency to reverse the trend of both children and adults away from the home in search of commercialised amusement and brings them back into the home for their fun'.[16] But, as happened earlier with radio, increasing material affluence led to an increase in the number of families possessing more than one television receiver, including portable models. The two-, three- and four-television set families have largely dispelled the earlier visions of a recreational renaissance within the family in the United States, and a similar process seems likely to happen in Britain.

Adequate research into the impact of television on the pattern of family leisure would have required a before-and-after study of particular types of family. In the absence of such research we are limited to fairly broad generalisations and some more or less informed speculations. For example, Kaplan guesses that the previous leisure resources and habits of the family were important factors in the amount and kind of television acceptance.[17] The family that in the past had chosen its reading, films and radio carefully would be likely to be equally discriminating with its television viewing. The family that in the past had to be entertained by outsiders would simply have followed through with television. In other families the advent of television probably made a real difference to the total pattern of their leisure, and certainly there is evidence that some kinds of programme stimulate participatory leisure activity in the arts and other spheres.

Several aspects of television are relevant to its effects on the family. Since it enters the privacy of the home, public control over its material is more sensitive than with other media. Peak viewing hours are in the later afternoon and evening, and so the home tends to become oriented to the demands of the programme schedule. Conflicts over programme preferences are likely to be most frequent in the one-set family; such conflicts need not happen in multiple-set families, but only because of the change from group to individual viewing. There is increasing indication that television is used as a pacifier or tranquilliser of children. In summing up the overall effect of these and other characteristics of television, Robert Williamson concludes that it has added more cohesion in the home than it has removed; despite its passivity, it has given a central pivot of values in the home, though probably below a desirable qualitative level.[18]

There are similar contradictory tendencies when we come to consider home-based recreation generally. The development of commercialised recreation has made it more difficult to preserve the values of family-made fun in the home. But, if the home is made a place where recreation opportunities are abundant, there is more chance of its members spending leisure time there. Although the housing shortage and relatively low standard of living in Britain have not made it possible for the average family home to include a games or recreation room, many families in the United States have been more fortunate in this respect. Even with restricted accommodation, however, a great many hobbies are carried on by individuals at home: reading, sketching, painting, caring for pets, making things of wood and other materials, collecting of all sorts, and many others.[19]

The pattern of contemporary family leisure activities that we have considered so far has been typical of Britain, the United States, and other advanced industrial societies. While many of the features noted may also be found to apply elsewhere, there are parts of the world where the present situation is different and where the rate and direction of change has been different. A full cross-cultural review of family leisure is not possible here, but one example may be given. In a study of the Kibbutz in Israel, Yonina Talman notes aspects of the decline of communal living.

'The tendency towards a more familistic pattern may be clearly discerned in the subtle transformation of informal relations and leisure-time activities of husband and wife. Free time spent in public has diminished considerably. . . . Spontaneous dancing and community singing sessions are rare. Husband and wife spend much of their free time together at home. . . . Much of the informal interchange between members occurs within the homes and entertaining and visiting are becoming joint family affairs.'[20]

Class differences in family leisure

Various enquiries on both sides of the Atlantic have concluded that social class membership has a considerable effect on the frequency with which different types of leisure activity are engaged in. Many of these 'class' influences on leisure may be seen as arising from the different types, circumstances and demands of work, and these were considered in Chapter 5. Here we are concerned more especially with the ways in which class (mediated by work, which in turn may be mediated by education) affects the family nature of leisure.

The picture is not a clear one, since various influences may pull in different directions. Take adequacy of living accommodation, for example. The typical middle-class home, more often than the typical working-class home, is likely to provide space for each individual to be alone, and space for the whole family to be together in reasonable comfort.[21] To some extent this will encourage the family members to spend their leisure in the home, though not necessarily in the home *together*. By contrast, the lower-income working-class family home is likely to be excessively crowded and therefore to be a less physically congenial place in which to spend leisure. With such homes, each individual may have to get out to be alone, or to do the things he or she wishes to do with friends. To the extent that such individuals do stay in the home, however, they are more likely to take part in 'family' leisure because shortage of space leaves them little option.

Leisure activities outside the home usually cost more (in travel, admission fees, etc.) than leisure spent inside the home. Cost is no doubt an important factor in explaining the greater participation rates of the middle class than the working class in nearly all forms of leisure activity. Many of the popular out-of-home forms of recreation, whether commercialised (the cinema, theatre, sports events) or social (golf, bridge, tennis, dinner parties) are designed primarily not for family-wide participation, but for individual or couple participation. Hence it may be said that the presence of children constitutes an interference with most of the recreation available to the middle-class father.[22] But this may be too harsh a judgement, since it fails to take into account the fact that playing with the children and helping to educate them can be part of the recreation or 'semi-leisure' available to a father. Also, middle-class fathers and mothers are more likely than those in lower socio-economic positions to be able to afford the services of a babysitter and hence to avoid too great a reduction in their own out-of-home leisure activities.

Summing up the recreation situation of what she calls 'lower middle-class' families in the United States, Betty Yorburg writes that they 'are not usually as lonely or isolated as the modern working class. Visiting as couples in the evening or coffee klatsching during the day, and the cooperative babysitting and other services, provide the functional equivalent of extended family activities and mutual aid for many residents of these burgeoning suburban communities.'[23] Traditionally, of course, it is the middle class in pursuit of individual self-advancement, rather than the working class in pursuit of solidarity, that has been 'lonely and isolated'. It may be that the modern working class, along with other groups in American society, is not too unhappy in its isolation from contemporary suburban community life.

Research in Britain suggests that the 'affluent worker' (i.e. a manual worker who can earn relatively high wages from long hours in a modern large-scale plant) has developed a 'privatised' style of life and leisure. The essential feature of this life-style is a pattern of social life which is centred on, and indeed largely restricted to, the home and the conjugal family. In one study, 62 per cent of all the weekend spare-time activities reported by workers and their wives took place in and about the home itself.[24] Other studies of leisure behaviour suggest that the degree of family involvement is more variable for the middle class. Some managers and professional employees 'work very long hours, spend a good deal of time travelling and do not necessarily share even their leisure with their families, much of it being spent with business colleagues'.[25] Other managers with less demanding work schedules are able to enjoy a variety of leisure activities, some with the family and some not. To quote two examples:

Family takes part:
'There's no question of tennis interfering with my family. I make sure it doesn't. My wife loves it and plays too, and our nine-year-old boy is keen.'
Family does not take part:
'I like sailing very much but my wife and daughter don't like it, so they're left behind. It means that I can't go as often as I'd like.'[26]

Leisure activities of the sexes

There are pronounced differences in the leisure patterns of males and females in our society. Many such differences reflect the differences in role which have historically been ascribed to men and women. The traditional, home-based existence of women, their lower educational status, their primary role as home-maker and mother, their second-class legal status, the comparatively sheltered condition of adolescent women and the differences in standards regarding sexual activity have all played a part in accounting for the difference in the leisure of women and men.

A wife usually has less free time than her husband, and during her leisure the wife's range of activities is more limited.[27] Time-budget research in twelve countries shows that married men have on average slightly more free time than married women, although single non-employed women have the greatest amount of free time.[28] Other research suggests that there is only one group of women who enjoy more leisure than their husbands: wives with dependent children who do no work outside the home. Wives who are employed spend more time on household chores than their husbands after finishing work, and therefore they have less time available for leisure. In the case of mothers with dependent children it appears that, whether they work outside the home or not, the demands of household duties leave them with less free time than their husbands.[29]

When the numbers of people involved in specific leisure interests are considered, it is men who usually predominate. For example, men more frequently attend sporting events and are involved in political associations. The church and various types of social club are, however, mainly supported by women, and especially by older women. Thus when all types of broadly defined leisure activity are taken into account, it seems that the difference between the sexes is not very wide. Also, as Roberts points out, it may be that women treat some of their household chores as leisure − cooking, for instance.[30] How long women spend on domestic work depends to a large extent on whether or not there is anything else that they would rather be doing. We should, therefore, be cautious about jumping to the conclusion that women are deprived of their fair share of leisure by the burden of looking after their families.

The leisure lives of husbands and wives is an important aspect of the whole conjugal relationship and of the pattern of marriage which they have chosen (or to which they feel they must conform). From this point of view, leisure is a direct function of family structure. The most important types of family structure are often called traditional or 'institution' and democratic or 'companionship'. In recent decades there has been a general move from the traditional to the democratic family, though at any one time the middle class will be found to have more democratic marriages than the working class. Bell and Healey describe the features of the traditional marriage which impinge on leisure.[31] It is based on rigid sex-role segregation, with the wife/mother contained within the domestic sphere and the husband concerned solely with extra-domestic economic and leisure activity – mutually exclusive worlds of 'men's work' and 'women's work'. All the interests of the husband are outside the home: his friends are all male and he associates with them in various clubs or pubs. His primary allegiance is to this peer group and all his leisure activities are carried out within it. For the woman in this type of marriage, the kitchen is entirely her place, which she occupies in the company of children or female kin, usually her mother. Such a woman's life is determined by domesticity, and her leisure is contained in the same way. Individual or non-domestic leisure is precluded by the rigid organisation of her life.

By contrast, the democratic marriage is based on the coming together of individual personalities free to express themselves within the context of consideration for other family members. Domestic activity and leisure are matters of accommodation to individual wishes, and marriage and family relationships are a creative, personal enterprise. Such a marriage releases the housewife for leisure, though at the cost of making less time available to the husband. It does not simply affect time available for leisure – it also creates values which make individual leisure part of the self-image of the marital partners. These values help to ensure an equitable distribution of the scarce resource of time between husband and wife. The relative affluence of most democratic families gives them a greater chance of getting functional support, such as baby-minding, which creates even more free time for individual or joint leisure by husband and wife.

One aspect of the division of leisure between the sexes in the democratic family is the extent to which the division may be blurring – a move, in fact, toward 'unisex' leisure. We have already noted in Chapter 4 the currently less marked distinction between boys' and girls' games than in the past. This process is also going on among adults. In the words of Kaplan, 'men are changing diapers, dabbling on the kitchen stove. . . . Women are wearing men's clothes in public without hesitation, playing golf, fixing home gadgets. . . .'[32] Men and women can with some impunity choose activities removed from former norms of propriety. She can fish as well as he; he can go to cookery classes as well as she. An element of freedom, a release from past traditions, has thus come into leisure for both sexes.

REFERENCES

1 R. O. Blood and D. M. Wolfe, *Husbands and Wives* (Glencoe, Free Press, 1960), pp. 147–8.
2 W. F. Ogburn and M. F. Nimkoff, *Technology and the Changing Family* (Boston, Houghton Mifflin, 1955), p. 130.
3 R. Fletcher, *The Family and Marriage in Britain* (Harmondsworth, Penguin Books, 1966), p. 194.
4 C. E. Vincent, 'Mental Health and the Family', *Marriage and the Family*, February 1967.
5 M. Kaplan, *Leisure in America* (New York, Wiley, 1960), p. 65.
6 J. S. Coleman, *The Adolescent Society* (New York, Free Press, 1961), p. 312.
7 R. G. Kraus, *Recreation and Leisure in Modern Society* (New York, Appleton-Century-Crofts, 1971), p. 347.
8 L. A. Zurcher and A. Meadow, 'On Bullfights and Baseball: An Example of Interaction of Social Institutions', *International Journal of Comparative Sociology*, March 1967.
9 N. Anderson, *Work and Leisure* (London, Routledge, 1961), p. 166.
10 Kaplan, *op. cit.*, p. 171.
11 R. Carlson *et al.*, *Recreation in American Life* (Belmont, Wadsworth, 1972), p. 15.
12 P. C. West and L. C. Merriam, 'Outdoor Recreation and Family Cohesiveness', *Journal of Leisure Research*, Autumn 1970.
13 C. S. Smith, 'Adolescence', in M. A. Smith *et al.*, eds, *Leisure and Society in Britain* (London, Allen Lane, 1973), p. 155.
14 British Travel Association–University of Keele, *Pilot National Recreation Survey*, Report No. 1, July 1967, p. 85.
15 B. Yorburg, *The Changing Family* (New York, Columbia University Press, 1973), p. 118.
16 R. E. Baber, *Marriage and the Family* (New York, McGraw-Hill, 1953, 2nd edn), pp. 264–5.
17 Kaplan, *op. cit.*, p. 67.
18 R. C. Williamson, *Marriage and Family Relations* (New York, Wiley, 1966), pp. 55–7.
19 W. B. Hallenbeck, *American Urban Communities* (New York, Harper, 1951), p. 465.
20 Y. Talmon, 'The Family in a Revolutionary Movement – The Case of the Kibbutz in Israel', in M. F. Nimkoff, ed., *Comparative Family Systems* (Boston, Houghton Mifflin, 1965), p. 276.
21 D. M. Schneider and R. T. Smith, *Class Differences and Sex Roles in American Kinship and Family Structures* (Englewood Cliffs, Prentice-Hall, 1973), p. 55
22 A. W. Green, 'The Middle Class Male Child and Neurosis', *American Sociological Review*, February 1946.
23 B. Yorburg, *op. cit.*, pp. 176–7.
24 J. H. Goldthorpe *et al.*, *The Affluent Worker in the Class Structure* (Cambridge, University Press, 1969), p. 102.
25 P. Willmott and M. Young, *Family and Class in a London Suburb* (London, Routledge, 1960), p. 20.
26 M. Young and P. Willmott, *The Symmetrical Family* (London, Routledge, 1973), pp. 232–3.

27   K. Roberts, *Leisure* (London, Longman, 1970), p. 42. See also Young and Willmott, *op. cit.*, p. 219.
28   A. Szalai, ed., *The Use of Time* (The Hague, Mouton), 1972.
29   British Broadcasting Corporation, *The People's Activities* (London, 1965).
30   Roberts, *op. cit.*, p. 43
31   C. Bell and P. Healey, 'The Family and Leisure', in M. A. Smith *et al.*, eds, *op. cit.*
32   Kaplan, *op. cit.*, p. 68.

Chapter 7

Leisure and Education

The amount and type of education we have influences the way we spend our leisure, the range of our activities, and whether these affect attainment in non-leisure spheres. There is an increasing tendency to define the aims of education broadly to include that of leading a full and satisfying leisure life. The practical side of this educational philosophy is to prepare young people in the schools for the kinds of leisure experience which are presently available to them and will be available in later life. A different type of link between education and leisure is seen in those learning activities which can be experienced as enjoyable ends in themselves. We shall look at the reasons for regarding education as something that should take place not just in schools or other educational institutions but as a life-long process.

The influence of education on leisure behaviour

Our schools, colleges and universities are organised on the implicit assumption that the educational task is primarily to prepare young people for a career, or at least a means of earning a living. The emphasis is on school *work* rather than on school *leisure*. Numbers of people have argued that the great emphasis on sports in schools militates against the achievement of academic goals. But some American research suggests that these fears may be misplaced.

Schafer and Armer questioned a sample of 585 boys attending, or who had recently left, two Midwestern high schools.[1] They found that the sportsmen performed academically on average *better* than the non-sportsmen. They also found that boys least likely to succeed academically, such as those with no aspirations for a college education, appeared to benefit most from participation in sports. The authors advance 'achievement motivation' as one possible explanation of this: a general desire for success may be reflected in either scholastic or sports achievement. Whether or not this is so, it is clear that to conceive of academic education and sporting (or, for that matter, other leisure) attainments as operating against each other is a false antithesis.

High levels of education have been found to stimulate participation in a wide variety of adult leisure activities. Surveys in both Britain and the United States show that interest and participation in many leisure activities, particularly the arts and cultural pursuits, are closely related to the amount of full-time education that people have received. The American study concluded that 'education findings reflect, in part, age and income differences . . . [but] education itself does have a distinct bearing on interest in outdoor recreation even after the influence of these other factors is taken into account'.[2] People with a similar education are much more likely to resemble one another in sporting habits, irrespective of class, than they are to resemble people of their own class with a different education.[3] Not all forms of sport and outdoor recreation are patronised more often by the better educated. Wrestling, for example, is more favoured by lower-status, less-educated people, and one survey showed that those who identified themselves as wrestling 'fans' had relatively low education compared to the larger audience.[4]

More generally, there can be little doubt that education has a marked influence in widening the span of the individual's wants.[5] But the widening is mainly in respect of those leisure activities which may be described as either more 'esoteric' or as more dependent on the middle-class values of individualism and rationality. Less demanding ways of spending leisure – generally, the more standardised products of the leisure industries – do not depend on (and may even be inhibited by) their patrons' having any particular level of education.

The impact of education seems to lie not so much in increasing opportunity to participate in leisure activities as in increasing awareness and desire. Swimming, for example, is a cheap pastime which is relatively unpopular among the lower income groups and the less well-educated. In the BTA/Keele survey about a quarter of those enjoying a high income and a university education mentioned swimming as one of their activities, but only 5–10 per cent at the other end of the scale.[6] Again, hiking requires little special equipment or expense, but is much more frequently pursued by those with more money and an advanced education.

The wider aims of education

One of the functions of leisure is to develop the personality, and in this sense the aims of leisure and the aims of education can come together. As Reynold Carlson puts it, 'the goals of recreation and education are not poles apart, since both are working toward enrichment of life for individuals. Learning is more rapid and lasting if it is pleasurable and satisfying in itself, and the finest educational experiences take on a recreational nature.'[7] A view of leisure which sees it, not as the opposite of work and of serious occupations, but as enabling these things to be freely undertaken is a view which has come to be held by many enlightened educators. The thought is well expressed by Sir Leon Bagrit: 'The whole purpose of leisure is to give people a chance of developing whatever talents and interests they have.'[8]

Part of education for leisure consists of attempting to instil in children (and hence in adults) ideas about what are deemed 'worthwhile' ways of spending leisure and what are not. Hence the persistent belief that such 'cultural' pursuits as drama, art and classical music must be 'laid on', because of the value they have as subjects, regardless of how people may use them or of what they may actually want. 'Art and culture were firmly separated from what the "mass" resorted to when it wished merely to be entertained: they could be identified instead with a small dominant social class, which could thus define their content, make them part of their own heritage and dispense them gratuitously to the deserving and worthy.'[9] As Augustine Basini puts it, the aims of education for leisure may be elite-oriented and reflect the norms and values of those holding economic and political power within a society.[10]

The growth of automation has led a number of commentators to foresee a shift of the emphasis of education away from the teaching of technical and other work skills and toward a teaching of competence in how to handle increasing amounts of leisure. Although the more optimistic forecasts of reduction in working time have yet to be realised, the thinking which relates education to leisure is still relevant, and likely to become more so in the future. As William Faunce puts it, 'in the long run, the primary responsibility of the schools may well become that of instilling certain kinds of values and interests which permit the creative use of leisure and, in general, the teaching not of vocational but of leisure skills'.[11]

Beyond fairly general statements about the desirability of a closer link between education and leisure, there is room for more than one view about the detailed working out of this process. For which kinds of leisure should we seek to educate people? How far can we – or should we – make the learning process a *playful* rather than a workmanlike experience? Should we attempt to 'educate' people to want and appreciate forms of leisure that we believe are good for them? These are difficult questions about which there is unlikely to be a consensus of opinion. Without trying to formulate all the relevant questions and answers, let us examine, in a little more depth, the views of two representative writers, one American and one British. These will give us some idea of the various considerations to be borne in mind when thinking about this complex subject.

Charles K. Brightbill has written several books on leisure, and in one of these he has a whole chapter on leisure and education.[12] He starts by inviting us to think of the latter not in the narrow fact-cramming, diploma-directed sense but rather in its deepest and best meaning – the *thinking* and *learning* process. If we are to have a flood of leisure, we must educate people for it. If we do not learn how to use the new leisure in wholesome, uplifting, decent, and creative ways, says Brightbill, we shall not live at all. This does not mean that leisure should be regimented. It is not so important that people use the parks, beaches, and libraries as it is that they learn to use their leisure in satisfying and creative ways – either with or without society's organised resources.

Brightbill believes that 'education for leisure' means exposing people early and long – in the home, the school and the community – to experiences that will help them develop appreciations and skills to use in increasingly available leisure time. He stresses that education for leisure is a slow, steady process, involving the imparting of skills and the readiness to exercise them. Leisure can contribute to other aims of education – to comprehending the world, attaining health and emotional stability, appreciating and expressing beauty. In this sense, leisure is not an escape from the toil of education – it is a revitalising element in the process of education itself. Brightbill is optimistic about the possibilities of educating for leisure, but thinks that 'the school will have to drop its traditional policy of isolating leisure education on the island of extra-curricular activities and bring it into the mainland of the school curriculum itself'.

James Simpson is a British educator whose views on leisure are similar in some ways to those of Brightbill and different from them in other ways.[13] He is on the whole less optimistic, and stresses more of the difficulties to be overcome than does Brightbill. He attaches importance to the function of education in enriching leisure by widening horizons of interest and enjoyment, and he writes about changing curricula in the schools to include leisure subjects. But he points to three 'dangers and difficulties' which beset the concept of education for leisure. The first is the putting of new labels on old bottles: the re-packing of existing curricula as 'education for life' or 'for maturity' without much change in the practice of educators. The second danger is paying too much attention to what surveys of leisure behaviour reveal, which tends to reduce education for leisure to the facilitation of mass trends which are often dictated by irresponsible interests. Thirdly we must, according to Simpson, beware of calling upon education to solve the 'problem of leisure'. The problem is not, contrary to forecasts, likely to be one of vast amounts of free time to fill, and those who worry about the quality of other people's leisure may simply be expressing their disappointment ('trivial', 'escapist', 'stultifying') with this.

Brightbill, Simpson and other writers agree that education does and should have a role to play in helping people to make better use of their leisure. The difficult question is how far educators should go in telling people what kind of leisure is good for them. Brightbill is typical of the more confident, convinced and moralistic school of thought which appeals to a consensus – one is tempted to say a 'silent majority' – on the subject of what is 'good' leisure. Simpson is more concerned to expose the bases of our moral judgements, and perhaps to be sceptical about how far we can truly 'forge out our own values'. Both views are fundamentally democratic, though Brightbill emphasises the provision of public services and voluntary contribution, while Simpson emphasises the linking of policies for improvement with the welfare and happiness of people individually and as a community. We should be thankful that there is open debate on this problem that admits of no single or easy answer.

Education for leisure

Having discussed some of the wider issues in education for leisure, we may now turn to the more concrete developments, proposals for further progress, and the problems involved. In the United States recreational activities now occupy an accepted place in the curricula of nearly all educational institutions and the trend in Britain is in the same direction. Subjects and activities of a recreational nature were initially incorporated into school life because it was believed that healthy recreation could produce beneficial moral effects, and because some influence over pupils' recreation made it easier to control their behaviour. Today, however, recreation is recognised as being desirable for its own sake, and most schools employ specialist staff to deal with this aspect of their work. Apart from learning sports, pupils can be introduced to literature, art, different types of music, handicrafts, and various other potentially satisfying leisure activities.[14]

Kenneth Roberts points out a number of factors that make it difficult for the schools to make much impact on their pupils' future leisure lives.[15] Many forms of recreation cannot be fully appreciated until people have attained physical, emotional, or social maturity. Developing an appreciation of literature amongst children, for instance, is extremely difficult. It is not easy for the educational system to impart a set of values that pupils will use continuously to structure their leisure lives as they mature into adulthood. Technological and social developments are continuously modifying the range of available leisure activities, making it difficult for the schools to prepare young people for their future leisure lives. In schools there tends to be an emphasis on organised competitive team games, but few adult leisure activities are of this kind. Finally, just as industrial recreation is shunned by many employees because it reminds them of work, so extra-curricular activities are shunned by many students (particularly the less successful ones) because they remind them of their school.

One of the major difficulties in framing a policy for education for leisure is how to make the content of the courses relevant to the lives and interests of the students within a context of preserving, and if possible enhancing, values which will be thought worthwhile by all concerned (in the long run, if not at the beginning). Richard Kraus thinks that 'if education is to be concerned with the recreational lives of students, it should prepare people to use their time wisely and constructively . . . there should be a direct concern with exploring the role of leisure in one's life. Schools should offer learning experiences in a wide variety of skills and interests useful in enriching lifelong recreational pursuits.'[16] Few would disagree with such a wide, varied and long-term policy, but we need to beware of adjectives like 'wisely' and 'constructively'. Who are we to say what it is 'wise' for someone else to do in his leisure, and is not 'constructive' a work term rather than a leisure term?

Again, a cautionary British view may be set against some excesses of American optimism and self-confident certainty. A. D. C. Peterson believes that 'we must admit that in the very assumption that education for leisure should take the form of arousing interest leading to enjoyment both in the arts and in sports, we are already involved in a value judgment. . . . If people prefer to work double shifts and buy a third television set for the bathroom, rather than to work single shifts and play string quartets or go sailing in their time off, have we any right as educators to try to change this pattern?'[17] The answer to this question is probably 'no' – educators do not have any such right, but they will no doubt continue to behave as if they had, because mankind has a long and sometimes noble history of efforts to 'improve' other people.

There are some precepts which derive from general educational principles but which apply in specific forms to leisure. Thus 'the need for developing sound judgment and good taste is vital'.[18] It is possible to hold that the cultivation of judgement and taste is desirable, while leaving room for individuals to disagree about the soundness of particular judgements and the goodness of particular tastes. This raises the question of uniformity in education generally and education for leisure in particular. Robert Frederick has traced the status of leisure-time (extra-curricular) activities in American public schools through at least four stages of development.[19] During the Colonial period an attitude of abstinence prevailed; children were expected to attend to their lessons. Then, during the decline of religious influence, there was tolerance of children organising their own dances, parties, etc. In the third period ('capitalisation') schools developed their own extra-curricular programmes, with expanding plant and staff. The fourth and contemporary period extends the third and is one of formalisation, including the assigning of academic credit to 'leisure' subjects.

Ronald Corwin criticises some of the effects of this formalisation.[20] Certain leisure activities have become standardised features of schooling, while others have been ignored. Struggles for favoured status have developed between the teachers responsible for various activities, such as the school band, athletic team or drama group. Once the activity is formalised, students sometimes are recruited for its benefit rather than their own. A prestige hierarchy of leisure-time activities develops from interdepartmental struggles, and from this hierarchy children learn which leisure activities are 'good', i.e. approved, and which are not. Perhaps the most serious criticism to be made of the present system is that formalisation of leisure encourages children to participate in uniform, recognised activities rather than to explore the multitude of alternative uses and conceptions of leisure. This uniformity leads people in later life to prefer *organised* leisure activities and to use leisure to escape from solitude and from themselves.

The way in which leisure subjects are taught in schools has also been criticised. There is a lack of teacher-training courses which include the implications of leisure for education. Those who defend the present content of teacher-training courses point out that material on education for leisure is included in other courses. But Corbin and Tait claim that 'emphasis in such courses has been placed upon perfection of performance rather than upon enjoyment of performance. When graduates of such courses enter the field of teaching, their methods are bound to be directed toward perfection rather than enjoyment.'[21] In music, art and dramatics particularly, Corbin and Tait believe that teaching should convey that these activities are fun and that everyone, not just a talented few, can take part.

Education as leisure

Implicit in what we have said so far is that, in addition to education being a preparation for leisure, the learning process itself can take on some of the characteristics of leisure. Traditionally, education has been equated with work. But among modern educators there is a growing realisation that both teaching and learning can be helpfully infused with qualities which we normally associate with leisure: spontaneity, the element of play, exchanging and evaluating ideas as ends in themselves rather than as a means to an end. With the advent of universal education, school children became an important part of the new leisure class, and public schools were among the first institutions to face the problems of leisure.[22] Free-moving, relaxed classrooms could not have been implemented if there had not been a basis for this in the wider society.

It is well known that play may assume creative roles in what may be called the self-education of the young.[23] The movement known as progressive education represents a means of adapting the schools to changing times. For many decades progressive educators have been pushing the idea that teaching methods must aim deliberately at feeding the impulse to intellectual as well as physical play, and that the child's impulses to 'experiment with life' should be taken as our guide in teaching him.[24] It would be rash to claim that these admirable precepts have been put into effect in more than a tiny minority of schools, but the few radical experiments have provided some interesting results and may point the way to what in the future will be more widely adopted in perhaps a modified form. Thus Anne Long writes of one programme, where a university professor was working with two primary school teachers to attempt to put across a mathematics programme the emphasis of which was on the fun of playing with and learning about numbers.[25]

The infusion of leisure into education is apparent not only at the school level but also at the adult education level. Some forms of non-vocational adult education – especially those concerned with the arts, humanities and social sciences – constitute a considerable leisure-time activity. The profession of adult education most closely resembles recreation in goals, organisation and method. There is often no line of demarcation indicating when the adult education sewing class or public-speaking club ceases to be adult education and becomes recreation, or vice versa. Generally speaking, if the activity is used for vocational progress, it is considered adult education. If it relates to skills and appreciations for use in leisure, it is recreation for adults.[26]

David Jary, in writing up his own survey of liberal adult education in Britain, argues that it is too often analysed as *education* producing extrinsic effects rather than as *leisure* yielding immediate gratifications.[27] The adult education movement has a traditional ideology of meeting social purposes through serious and sustained study. But, contrary to this ideology, Jary's survey of students' reasons for attending courses shows that they are primarily a leisure-centred activity. Informal teaching methods, extensive class participation, and particularly lengthy discussion periods are typical features. Subjects such as English literature, history and sociology are treated in a manner quite different from that in undergraduate education.

They are mined for their general relatedness to life, and above all for their personal relevance. They are used as prompts for generalised reflection and discussion, and the heart and life of the whole activity is the immediate pleasure of the class.

Jary concludes that the leisure-centredness of liberal adult education ought not to be hidden or apologised for. It should be recognised and its gratifications elaborated. It should be seen as a highly distinctive form of leisure.

Life-long education

The idea that education is a permanent process, and not something that takes place only at relatively early stages of life, is slowly gaining ground and is fully consonant with an appreciation of the relationship between education and leisure. At each stage of the life-cycle, education has a role to play in preparing the individual to make the best possible use of his leisure time. In school, college and university he can learn about the range of choices available and experiment with as many particular activities as he wishes. In adult life there are many opportunities for learning new skills to be used in leisure pursuits and (as we have seen) for experiencing the process of learning itself as a pleasurable and sociable activity. In preparation for retirement courses the emphasis is on introducing the individual to an extended and appropriate range of leisure opportunities, some of which he may be able to take up or extend when he finishes his life's work. Finally, during the period of retirement, education can continue to offer the individual the mental stimulation which is so important in averting senility. When employment comes to an end, when children have grown and departed and domesticity becomes a settled routine, when relaxing entertainments begin to pall, mind and body may crave some purposeful and enjoyable leisure pursuit which education will facilitate.[28]

The campaign for life-long education is part of a broader movement for flexible life-styles which aims at personal growth throughout life, and which requires social and economic policies that provide adults of all ages with a range of options for work, education, and free-time activities.[29] The lack of education and stimulating work may, indeed, narrow the range of leisure opportunities which the individual sees open to him. Harold Wilensky has observed that 'among men not accustomed to the wider universe made available by demanding work, it takes a long, expensive education to avoid an impoverished life'.[30] We have to admit that leisure in modern society has for most people become commercialised and circumscribed by habit. There is little spontaneous creativeness, while standards of opportunities offered, for instance, for the enjoyment of music or the drama, are potentially far greater than they have ever been.[31]

It is sometimes claimed that the idea of linking education with leisure will only appeal to a minority of persons, and that others will continue to view education narrowly as preparation for work. Thus John Johnstone asserts that the typical lower-class person does not think of education in terms of personal growth or self-realisation, and as a consequence is even less ready to turn to adult education for recreational purposes than he is for purposes of vocational advancement.[32] But to say this is to underestimate the extent to which 'lower-class' is the result of lower education. As the general level of education in our society improves, it is likely that more people will pursue a pattern of life which includes leisure activities that are instructive but at the same time are a source of satisfaction and pleasure for themselves. This is the pattern which Frances Noe reminds us is typical of adolescence in some pre-industrial societies.[33] The accommodation of recreational activities to serious matters permits learning within a festive situation.

Until fairly recently, most societies were too poor to be able to afford the formal education beyond childhood of more than a minority of their members. Today, the economically advanced countries of the world *could* afford a longer and more leisure-oriented education for all of their members, if sufficient importance were attached to it. Arnold Toynbee quotes the example of Denmark, where high schools are for grown-ups, not for children. 'A Danish farmer will save money for years to enable himself to take a six-months' or a twelve-months' course, and he will make it a point of honour to choose his subject with an eye to raising the level of his culture and not with an eye to improving his economic position.'[34] To give more people such opportunities we would need to make our schools and other educational institutions year-round operations with increased continuing educational opportunities for all age groups. As Corbin and Tait remark, we learn at all ages, and the idea of teaching for future use should be replaced with the pattern of continuing education for all throughout the year.[35]

REFERENCES

1 W. E. Schafer and J. M. Armer, 'On Scholarship and Interscholastic Athletics', in E. Dunning, ed., *The Sociology of Sport* (London, Cass, 1971).
2 Outdoor Recreation Resources Review Commission, *Outdoor Recreation for America* (Washington, US Government Printing Office, 1962).

3   T. Cauter and J. S. Downham, *The Communication of Ideas* (London, Chatto & Windus, 1954), p. 80.

4   G. P. Stone, 'Wrestling – The Great American Passion Play', in E. Dunning, ed., *op. cit.*

5   J. K. Galbraith, *The Affluent Society* (London, Hamish Hamilton, 1958), p. 217.

6   British Travel Association–University of Keele, *Pilot National Recreation Survey*, 1967.

7   R. Carlson *et al.*, *Recreation in American Life* (Belmont, Wadsworth, 1972), p. 13.

8   Sir L. Bagrit, *The Age of Automation* (London, Weidenfeld & Nicolson, 1965), p. 48.

9   B. D. Davies and A. Gibson, *The Social Education of the Adolescent* (University of London Press, 1967), p. 44.

10 A. Basini, 'Education for Leisure: A Sociological Critique', in J. T. Haworth and M. A. Smith, eds, *Work and Leisure* (London, Kimpton, 1975).

11 W. A. Faunce, 'Automation and Leisure', in H. B. Jacobson and J. S. Roucek, eds, *Automation and Society* (New York, Philosophical Library, 1959), p. 305.

12 C. K. Brightbill, *The Challenge of Leisure* (Englewood Cliffs, N.J., Prentice-Hall, 1960).

13 J. Simpson, 'Education for Leisure', in M. A. Smith *et al.*, eds, *Leisure and Society in Britain* (London, Allen Lane, 1973).

14 K. Roberts, *Leisure* (London, Longman, 1970), p. 116.

15 *Ibid.*, pp. 117–19.

16 R. G. Kraus, *Recreation and Leisure in Modern Society* (New York, Appleton-Century-Crofts, 1971), p. 15.

17 A. D. C. Peterson, *The Future of Education* (London, Cresset, 1968), p. 18.

18 H. Dan Corbin, *Recreation Leadership* (Englewood Cliffs, N. J., Prentice-Hall, 1970, 3rd edn), p. 79.

19 R. W. Frederick, *The 3rd Curriculum: Student Activities in American Education* (New York, Appleton-Century-Crofts, 1959).

20 R. G. Corwin, *A Sociology of Education* (New York, Appleton-Century-Crofts, 1965), pp. 88–94.

21 H. D. Corbin and W. J. Tait, *Education for Leisure* (Englewood Cliffs, N.J., Prentice-Hall, 1973), p. 61.

22 Corwin, *op. cit.*, p. 86.

23 N. Anderson, *Work and Leisure* (London, Routledge, 1961), p. 132.

24 T. Percy Nunn, *Education: Its Data and First Principles* (London, Arnold, 1929), p. 87.

25 A. Long, 'The New School – Vancouver', in B. and R. Gross, eds, *Radical School Reform* (New York, Simon & Schuster, 1969), p. 292.

26 R. Carlson *et al.*, *op. cit.*, p. 13.

27 D. Jary, 'Evenings at the Ivory Tower: Liberal Adult Education', in Smith *et al.*, eds, *op. cit.*, p. 263.

28 B. Groombridge, *Education and Retirement* (London, National Institute of Adult Education, 1960), p. 18.

29 R. J. Havighurst *et al.*, 'Work, Leisure and Education: Toward the Goal of Creating Flexible Life Styles', *The Gerontologist*, Winter 1969.

30 H. L. Wilensky, 'Mass Society and Mass Culture: Independence or Interdependence?', *American Sociological Review*, April 1964.

31 K. Mannheim and W. A. C. Stewart, *An Introduction to the Sociology of Education* (New York, Humanities Press, 1962), p. 149.

32 J. W. C. Johnstone, 'Leisure and Education in Contemporary American

Life', Boston University, Centre for the Study of Liberal Education for Adults, Notes and Essays on Education for Adults, No. 43, 1964.

33 F. P. Noe, 'A Pre-industrial Examination of Adolescent Leisure in a Cross-cultural Setting', *Adolescence*, Autumn 1971.

34 Quoted in R. Gross, ed., *The Teacher and the Taught* (New York, Dell, 1963).

35 Corbin and Tait, *op. cit.*, p. 156.

Chapter 8

Leisure and Religion

The secular convention of taking holidays originated as the religious custom of observing holy days, and there have been various attempts to integrate religion with both leisure and play. Leisure has an affinity with religion in a number of ways: both express the desire for personal well-being, afford opportunities to exercise free will, are integrative and inclusive, and attach special significance to re-creation. The type of religious belief prevalent in a community influences the opportunities for leisure both of the faithful and of the public at large. Despite the general decline of religious belief and observance, the various churches and other religious bodies play a substantial part in providing organised leisure facilities for large numbers of people, particularly the young. Finally, some phases of religion itself may be seen (at least by the outside observer) to take on the character of leisure activities.

Holy days, holidays and celebrations

There is nothing new about holidays; they are found in all cultures. In AD 321 the Emperor Constantine, without reference to any Christian ideals, ordered Sunday to be a public holiday.[1] Christmas and Easter are examples of holidays which originated as religious ceremonials, but many harvest and spring festivals are much older.[2] In medieval Europe, dominated by Catholicism, about one day in three was a holiday of some kind. Many of the saints' days which Catholicism had fostered were abandoned after the Reformation. This was part of what Robert Malcolmson calls the hostile disposition toward recreational practices associated with Protestantism. He writes of the dissatisfaction which developed with the manner in which popular recreations were customarily observed:

'Much of this dissatisfaction with traditional recreations was generated by the movement of dissident puritanism . . . the traditions of popular leisure were objectionable on a number of grounds: they were thought to be profane and licentious – they were occasions of worldly indulgence which tempted men from a godly life; being rooted in pagan and popish practices, they were rich in the sort of ceremony and ritual which poorly suited the Protestant conscience; they frequently involved a desecration of the Sabbath and an inter-ference with the worship of the true believers; they disrupted the peaceable order of society, distracting men from their basic social duties – hard work, thrift, personal restraint, devotion to family, a sober carriage.'[3]

Puritanism was always a minority movement, however, and its more extreme views on leisure were uncongenial to the bulk of the population. Popular recreations remained socially functional: holidays, for instance, provided psychological counterweights to the burden of sustained labour. In eighteenth-century England the Church was only peripherally involved in the traditional festivities of the workers. But in much of Catholic Europe the Church's participa-tion in these festivities remained vigorous; holidays were still in some measure holy days, and the Church continued a holiday calendar which was very much of its own making. By contrast, in England, where the Church was more subservient to the government, much of the religious significance of the periodic festivals had been swept away during the sixteenth and seventeenth centuries.[4] Conflicts over recreation deeply influenced popular attitudes to religion and probably accelerated the process of secularisation. Religion and recreation had once been closely integrated, but by the nineteenth century they were beginning to compete, not only for people's time but also in values.[5]

Max Kaplan illustrates how, during American history, the Church has attempted to assume control over non-work time.[6] As with Britain and continental Europe, there was a substantial variation between places and over time in the religious influence on leisure behaviour. In seventeenth-century Virginia, for example, laws and sanctions against such leisure pursuits as gaming and drinking were fully as restrictive as those in New England. But whereas later Virginians were more generally permitted to make the most of whatever opportunities for recreation their expanding life presented, in New England the stern rule of Calvinism held its ground more firmly. The magistrates attempted to suppress almost every form of recreation long after the practical justification for such an unrelenting attitude had disappeared. An uncharitable view of such a history of implacable opposition to most forms of leisure and recreation is, according to Kaplan, to declare that the Church leaders were narrow, bigoted, inhuman and fanatic. A more understanding view is to note that in a frontier society men who guard the religion must be strong men, and commands must be stark and sharp.

As society became more settled and complex, the earlier black-and-white religious attitudes to work and play gave way to a more subtle, intellectual and theological approach. Also, there were some minority religions which had never taken a puritanical attitude to leisure. For example, W. Seward Salisbury writes of the Mormons, who are strong advocates of physical exercise and wholesome recreation and 'have from early days put a high value on play and joy while at the same time repudiating the religious pessimism and blue law orientation of the Puritan tradition. . . . The Mormons, in short, have spiritualized recreation.'[7]

Within the last generation or so there have been significant attempts to reconcile both play and leisure with religion. The historian Johan Huizinga has suggested that play and religion share a number of common qualities.[8] First, both have the possibility of seriousness and are imbued with ideals of perfection. Second, both relate to physical space that is finite but unbounded in the imagination (playing and praying take place in worlds of their own rules and sanctions). Third, the holy and the make-believe are both symbolic, making use of pageantry, special clothing and language. In some respects such an analogy between play and religion may seem forced, although it is certainly instructive to note the similarities between *some* forms of play and *some* aspects of religion.

Probably the most ambitious attempt to integrate leisure with religion was made by the Swiss Catholic philosopher Josef Pieper. He noted that 'the Christian and Western conception of the contemplative life is closely linked to the Aristotelean notion of leisure'.[9] For Pieper, leisure 'is a mental and spiritual attitude – it is not simply the result of external factors, it is not the inevitable result of spare time, a holiday, a week-end or a vacation. It is . . . an attitude of mind, a condition of the soul, and as such utterly contrary to the ideal of "worker". . . .'[10] He also attaches great spiritual and even therapeutic value to celebrations and festivals, though clearly his identification of 'leisure' with 'festival' places a very narrow meaning on the former term, and is reminiscent of Aristotle's restriction of 'leisure' to music and contemplation: 'In celebrating, in holding festivals upon occasion, man experiences the world in an aspect other than the everyday one. The festival is the origin of leisure and the inward and ever-present meaning of leisure . . . if real leisure is deprived of the support of genuine feast-days and holy-days, work itself becomes inhuman. . . .'[11]

The affinity of leisure and religion

We have considered above some of the conscious attempts to reconcile leisure (or at least some aspects of leisure) with religion. It is also possible to discern similarities between these two spheres of life and society which derive from a comparison of what each aims to achieve and of what each offers the individual.

Our first theme is that both leisure and religion express the desire for personal well-being and self-realisation. It must be admitted that this correspondence rests upon a particular conception of leisure – essentially the normative or subjective one favoured by men of religion, philosophers and educators – and upon a particular function of leisure: that of personal development. The spirit of leisure, according to Robert Lee, is the spirit of learning, of self-cultivation.[12] In our present society, which contains increasing numbers of people who are concerned with how leisure is spent, religious thinking, whatever the faith, tends to accept free time as a potential period of spiritual growth. 'Leisure is the occasion for the development of broader and deeper perspective and for renewing the body, mind and spirit. . . . Leisure provides the occasion for learning and freedom for growth and expression, for rest and restoration, for rediscovering life in its entirety.'[13] Such a conception of leisure brings it close to a conception of the religious life in both its active and contemplative aspects.

A second and related theme is that leisure and religion are both spheres which afford opportunities to exercise free will and express our inner desires. 'Each places us at the centre of our own destiny and each recognises the supreme worth of the individual. In a very real sense, religion and leisure are existential in nature through the margin they provide to exercise free will. Everybody must be his own expert in the spiritual and leisurely life.'[14] Of course, this last statement by Brightbill must not be taken too literally: the kind of spiritual and leisurely life which we work out for ourselves is to a large extent the product of the particular social influences to which we have been subject. All religions have their spiritual guides and, more recently, it has been thought to be appropriate to train 'leisurists', 'recreators', etc. to act as leisure experts and leaders. Nevertheless, it is fair to say that the freedom of the individual *is* of concern to many of those who prescribe for our spiritual and leisurely needs. And sometimes the constraints are the reality and the freedom merely the promise. In this vein, Gordon Dahl writes: 'The leisure that people need today is not free time but a free spirit; not more hobbies or amusements but a sense of grace and peace which will lift us beyond our busy schedules.'[15]

Leisure and religion share a third characteristic of being integrative and inclusive, though again we must stress that this depends upon a broad rather than a narrow conception of the scope of each, and particularly of leisure. Following Pieper, Dahl believes that leisure is essentially spiritual and that it 'is man's synthesizing factor in a "component" civilization'.[16] Changing to more popular language, he adds that leisure means 'getting it all together' in a new and better way. This would appear to involve taking a religious attitude to leisure, as illustrated by the question posed and answered by Max Kaplan: 'How can religion put morals into something that at first sight seems far removed from the central stream of daily life? Obviously by calling attention to the fact that all of life is one, interrelated and inseparable, if not on social or economic levels, then on the psychological.'[17] If we accept the double proposition that religious morality is most concerned with the 'central stream of daily life' and that we are moving toward a more leisure-centred society, then the role of religion in leisure may increase rather than decrease. Certainly the subject of leisure seems to be gaining more of the attention of religious writers, and in a more constructive and less censorious spirit, than formerly.

A fourth meeting-ground of leisure and religion is in the understanding of what is meant by 're-creation'. While this is not the place to attempt a full analysis of 'creation and recreation' as the religious equivalents of the secular 'work and leisure', it is worth asking why recreation is so often used as a synonym for leisure. Literally, recreation refers to the apparent purpose of leisure activity, a therapeutic process of repairing the wear and tear resulting from work and its stresses. By 'recreation' we must mean to restore, to re-establish, to return to an original or ideal state. What is that ideal state? According to Ralph Glasser, religion offered an answer in the idea of Grace, a spiritual unity with the Divine Will, inseparable from a certain kind of conduct.[18] Separated from this spiritual view, the idea of recreation has the aimless circularity of simply restoring us to a state in which we can best continue our work.

Religious prescriptions for leisure

The followers of most religions find that, in varying degrees, they are expected to conform in spirit and in action to certain precepts about how leisure time should be spent. Established religions are also able to exert a restrictive influence on the ways in which members of the general public are able to spend their leisure, though this influence is less today than it was in the past. We shall examine both these aspects.

Given that the necessary data were available, it would be possible to analyse how each religious body has prescribed for the leisure and recreative life of its faithful. Rather than attempt this huge task, even in general terms, for a number of the many religions known to man, we may take two examples, one from an advanced industrial society and one from a largely peasant economy.

Bryan Wilson has made a sociological study of three religious sects in Britain.[19] One of these is the Elim Foursquare Gospel Church, a pentecostal, evangelical and revivalist body, which in 1954 claimed 250 churches in the British Isles, though this figure has probably been reduced subsequently. In a chapter devoted to the social teachings and practices of Elim, Wilson suggests that these follow a form of other-worldly asceticism. No stricture is made on labour and money earning, since these are taken to be simple economic necessities. But the use to which income is put, and the expenditure of leisure time, is the sphere in which the evangelist feels himself most competent to judge.

Leisure habits are the particular area of life in which the Elimites most see the danger of 'worldly' activity. They accept a narrowly recreative function of leisure: 'time spent playing games, reading and walking is not wasted if we go back to our work benefited in soul and body'.[20] But the engagement in spare-time activity which is not in some sense associated with religion tends to incur disapproval. In this respect the Elim movement reflects the puritanical Methodism of a hundred or more years ago. Smoking and drinking are frowned upon, the latter more than the former because it is held to be a social more than a personal habit. Gambling and swearing are proscribed; but modern media of entertainment have posed some problems. Evangelistic bodies like the Elim have found it less easy to condemn the radio than the dance hall, and television less easy to condemn than the theatre.

A very different example of religious influence on leisure patterns of the faithful is seen in the Mexican institution of bullfighting. Florence Kluckhohn describes the typical Mexican's passive dependence upon the saints and submissive and accepting attitude toward the supernatural.[21] This ties in with features of the bullfight itself: the domination of the bull by the matador, and the submissive behaviour the latter expects from his assistants. Institutional leisure behaviour may thus exhibit similar features to organised religion, since the same basic cultural values run through all of a society's institutions.

Religious prescriptions for leisure may also affect the public at large, many of whom do not subscribe to the religious beliefs which effectively restrict their leisure behaviour. The outstanding example of this is the Sabbatarian movement, directed at the careful regulation of social behaviour on Sundays.[22] The Lord's Day Observance Act of 1780, drawn up by the Bishop of London, severely limited Sunday trade, and all places of entertainment which demanded payment were to be closed. Later legislation in Britain closed public houses on a

Sunday and prohibited trading in connection with newspapers, shaving, smoking, etc.

Since the end of the last century Sabbatarian legislation has, however, tended to weaken. In modern industrial societies Sunday is generally viewed as a day of pleasure and relaxation free from work. It has become widely recognised that modern man needs a fixed and sufficient time for leisure.[23] Moreover, the arrangement whereby this time for leisure is fixed for an entire day and on the same day for everybody has one important advantage over all proposals for a staggered working week: that of making it easy for members of a family or friends and acquaintances to see one another during their leisure time. Among other factors which have aided the recognition of Sunday as a day of leisure are: the general acceptance of watching television on Sunday; the increasing opportunities to find relaxation and pleasure in travel, including visiting; the extension of Sunday to the two-day weekend (the French speak of 'the week with two Sundays'); and the sharing of the more permissive attitude to Sunday leisure by church congregations as well as the general public.

Religion and organised leisure

Although, as we saw earlier, it is possible to reconcile the spirit of religion with the spirit of play, a reconciliation of religion with many organised forms of leisure is not so easy. For example, games, as Kaplan points out, are essentially a secular pursuit, and can become a substitute for religion.[24] In Europe and America the Church has traditionally either condemned games outright or at least sought to control them. The strongest religious opposition is reserved for games of chance. Kaplan reasons that this is because in games like bingo and cards the luck of winning is uncontrollable whereas, in contrast, God is not fickle, for he establishes an order with cause and effect. Religious ideology, based on merited reward and punishment, cannot permit luck to become a powerful ideology. Under secular pressure, some churchmen have, in fact, come to terms with some forms of gambling, even using them in raising money for the Church. This, however, has tended to create a division of opinion within the ranks of supporters of the Church.

As a community institution, the Church has taken on elements of a social centre. This is one of the ways in which it accommodates itself to the realities of contemporary life. Both Catholics and, to a lesser extent, Protestants seek to ensure that their young people will meet other young people through the Church, the sociability of the group being 'wholesome', somewhat planned, and the content of meetings consonant with Christian teachings.[25] Richard Kraus describes the approach to leisure and recreation taken by these organisations formed with religious aims, such as the Young Men's and Women's Christian Associations.[26] Rather than attempting to repress 'sinful' forms of play, they instead seek to promote joyous and affirmative programmes of participation. They see leisure and the creative recreational involvement of young people as having great potential for their total growth, both social and spiritual.

A different way in which religion relates to organised leisure is involved in the claim that certain sports are the equivalent of a surrogate or secular religion. This may apply to almost any sport which inspires the devotion of large numbers of players or spectators, which has its own rituals, hero-worship, and so on. Thus Morris R. Cohen makes the following case for baseball in the United States to be regarded as a national religion:

'The essence of religious experience, so we are told, is the "redemption from the limitations of our petty individual lives and the mystic unity with a larger life of which we are part". And is this not precisely what the baseball devotee or fanatic, if you please, expresses when he watches the team representing his city battling with another? . . . Careful students of Greek civilization do not hesitate to speak of the religious value of the Greek drama . . . baseball exercises and purifies all of our emotions, cultivating hope and courage when we are behind, resignation when we are beaten, fairness for the other team when we are ahead, charity for the umpire, and above all the zest for combat and conquest.'[27]

This is perhaps a somewhat idealised picture of the feelings of the average baseball fan, but it is the sort of heroic myth which is part of the sporting scene in contemporary America.

To quote the case of another sport, Edgell and Jary have shown how the game of association football ('soccer') has many features similar to those of a religion.[28] Football grounds can possess the aura of a church. A sports writer expresses a common feeling when he says: 'Whenever I arrive at any football ground, or merely pass close to one when it is silent, I experience a unique alerting of the senses. The movement evokes my past in an instantaneous rapport which is more certain, more secret, than memory.' Professional players who write biographies report a similar sense of awe on entering football grounds, and this bears testimony to the 'religious' quality of the meaning of the game. Ritual and ceremony are other analogies: football has chantings and 'responses'. Edgell and Jary conclude that a full argument for football as a religion would stress not only its function in providing integration with a particular group or nation, but also its capacity to generate a wider, more universal sense of shared humanity and 'the ultimate'.

Organised leisure is a mode of filling the non-work time of the mass of people, and in modern industrial societies religious activities have to compete for this time. As part of his theme of America and other countries as 'time famine' cultures, Staffan Linder quotes a number of examples of ways in which increasing pressure of time has adversely affected religious life.[29] Not only are there fewer religious holidays, but there tend to be shorter and less frequent religious services. Swedish sermons are advertised as 'of reasonable length' and thus 'adapted to the modern individual'. Of a Canadian church service it was recorded that 'The moment the last prayer was said, everyone stood up and seemed in a great hurry to leave . . . there was little loitering or conversation and everyone seemed instead to head straight for his car and drive away.'

Religion as leisure activity

The competition that religious activities have to meet from other ways of spending time in a time-famine and consumption-oriented society brings us to the proposition that religion itself may be a form of leisure activity. This theme is part of a broader consideration of the extent of differentiation between religious and secular activities at different historical periods and in different places. In medieval times it may be said that everything people did was 'steeped in religion' but this did not necessarily mean disciplined solemnity. As Elias and Dunning sum it up, 'in the folk societies of the middle ages, secular activities were more religious and religious activities more secular than in contemporary societies'.[30]

On the specific question of church-sponsored leisure activities in America, it appears that considerable changes have taken place over time. Taking the Midwest area as an example, a study carried out a decade or so ago indicated that almost all the churches held special extra-church activities, such as bazaars, church dinners, special lectures, festivals and the like from time to time.

'If historical records can be trusted, one would infer that in earlier periods such activities were very important, not only in the life of the church, but also in the life of the community as a whole. Their importance today seems to be much less . . . [the data] suggest that these activities were much more widespread in rural areas and among Catholics than in larger communities and among Protestants.'[31]

Meyer Nimkoff shows that the Negro church is an important and approved medium of sociability and entertainment.

'The church is the place to meet one's friends of both sexes. For young people, its value here is less seasonal than that of the school.

Debating societies, tea parties, guilds, clubs, class meetings, and many other activities constitute a rich offering of social activities. . . . The Negro church thus provides a larger number of functions and a fuller expression than the white church.'[32]

In simpler societies it is possible to see the way in which an imported religion can be adapted to the more leisurely life of the people. Thus Nels Anderson quotes the case of Trinidad natives who accepted the religion offered by the missionaries but rejected the dignified British way of worship.

'For them the holy spirit did not merely abide within, it had to become active and vocal. The natives would jump and shout. . . . The shouting religious meeting assumes the character of a dance with singing, jumping, handclapping and emotional display. The sexes come into close smiling "brother and sister" contact, religious ceremony shakes free of conventional stiffness to become play, and the assembly becomes a happy leisure-time activity.'[33]

The religion does not have to be imported to show leisurely qualities. Sylvia Vatuk describes the neighbourhood devotional singing which takes place in some white-collar parts of North India: 'The general atmosphere is reverent and pious, but the occasion is nonetheless regarded as a social one, an opportunity to meet with friends and catch up on recent events in their families and in the neighbourhood.'[34] In continental Europe and away from the big cities, elements of play – fireworks, dancing, 'fun' music – are clearly visible in many 'religious' processions.[35]

In advanced industrial societies, it is not difficult to show that contemporary institutional religion possesses certain social qualities which allow participants to see it as a somewhat sedate form of leisure-time pursuit. W. Pickering gives evidence that for many people attending church is akin to going to the cinema or the theatre, attending evening classes or visiting one's friends.[36] The churches have tacitly encouraged worshippers to find pleasure in what they were doing – in the singing of hymns, in listening to self-confirming sermons, in hearing organ voluntaries, solo singing and choral works. This development is the outcome of the churches' finding themselves to be one of a very large number of voluntary organisations competing for people's time and commitment, though it is not suggested that every religious act or belief can be viewed as having leisure-time connotations.

Alain Touraine goes some way towards agreeing with Pickering's point of view. Religion, he maintains, becomes a leisure activity, that is deliberate, unregulated behaviour, personal and secret.[37] However, he intends not to equate religious life with particular leisure activities, but to 'recognise in all the aspects of culture the same general evolution that casts light on the profound meaning of leisure activity: the passage from socially and morally regulated leisure behaviour to action freely oriented toward objects or values that are all the more demanding of the individual to the degree that they are no longer separated from him by a labyrinth of social codes'.

The recent growth of popular forms of religion owes much to the ways in which they have taken advantage of the appeal of excitement and the collective search for identity, a twin appeal not dissimilar from that offered by more overt leisure pursuits. Orrin Klapp has drawn attention to the remarkable growth during the twentieth century of interest in activities best described as cultic.[38] Some of these activities are 'fringe' religion: mysticism, magic, spiritualism, Zen Buddhism, and new sects of all kinds. Jehovah's Witnesses, for example, grew from 60,000 to 950,000 in twenty years. There is a tremendous sale of religious and inspirational literature. Billy Graham fills stadiums with over 30,000 'enquirers' at a time. Theologians greet such a religious boom with misgivings, wondering if it is Christian, wondering if it is even religion.

Klapp believes that widespread interest in new cults is a response to emptiness or 'sickness' of meaning in the existing order – and the churches are part of this existing order. Banality has crept into conventional religious life: congregations are bored, church services have become rationalistic, bureaucratic, filled with the spirit of business; the mystery has gone, they really have no Grail. (It should be noted that this analysis disagrees with, or ignores, Pickering's claim of a leisure-oriented religion – though it may be that the sickness is in conventional leisure, too.) By contrast, new cults offer excitement and hope. Organisations like the Shriners, with their costume, trappings, pageantry, high jinks and secret ritual, have a buffering function to protect their members from the meaninglessness of society-at-large. If all this is true, then religion will successfully compete with spontaneous and collective forms of leisure only where it meets the same human needs: for meaning, and a sense of identity.

REFERENCES

1 W. Rordorf, *Sunday* (London, SCM Press, 1968), p. 162.
2 N. Anderson, *Work and Leisure* (London, Routledge, 1961), p. 107. See also S. Gordon, *Holidays* (London, Batsford, 1972), pp. 7–9.
3 R. W. Malcolmson, *Popular Recreations in English Society 1700–1850* (Cambridge, University Press, 1973), p. 6.

4 *Ibid.*, pp. 13, 14, 74.
5 B. Harrison, 'Religion and Recreation in Nineteenth Century England', *Past and Present*, December 1967.
6 M. Kaplan, *Leisure in America* (New York, Wiley, 1960), pp. 151–2.
7 W. S. Salisbury, *Religion in American Culture* (Homewood, Ill., Dorsey, 1964), p. 184.
8 J. Huizinga, *Homo Ludens* (London, Routledge, 1949), pp. 18–27.
9 J. Pieper, *Leisure the Basis of Culture* (London, Faber, 1952), p. 23.
10 *Ibid.*, p. 43.
11 *Ibid.*, pp. 45, 63.
12 R. Lee, *Religion and Leisure in America* (Nashville, Abingdon, 1964), p. 33.
13 *Ibid.*, pp. 34–5.
14 C. K. Brightbill, *The Challenge of Leisure* (Englewood Cliffs, N.J., Prentice-Hall, 1960), p. 38.
15 G. J. Dahl, *Time, Work and Leisure* (Christian Century Foundation, 1971), p. 187.
16 G. J. Dahl, *Work, Play and Worship in a Leisure-Oriented Society* (Minneapolis, Augsburg, 1972), p. 74.
17 Kaplan, *op. cit.*, p. 150.
18 R. Glasser, 'Leisure and the Search for a Satisfying Identity', in M. A. Smith *et al.*, eds, *Leisure and Society in Britain* (London, Allen Lane, 1973), p. 64.
19 B. R. Wilson, *Sects and Society* (London, Heinemann, 1961).
20 *Ibid.*, p. 80.
21 F. Kluckhohn and F. L. Strodbeck, *Variations in Value Orientations* (New York, Row, Peterson, 1961), p. 235.
22 W. S. F. Pickering, 'The Secularized Sabbath', in M. Hill, ed., *A Sociological Yearbook of Religion in Britain*, No. 5 (London, SCM Press, 1972), p. 34.
23 Rordorf, *op. cit.*, p. 300.
24 Kaplan, *op. cit.*, p. 157.
25 *Ibid.*, pp. 177–8.
26 R. G. Kraus, *Recreation and Leisure in Modern Society* (New York, Appleton-Century-Crofts, 1971), p. 82. See also H. D. Corbin and W. J. Tait, *Education for Leisure* (Englewood Cliffs, N.J., Prentice-Hall, 1973), pp. 123–5.
27 M. R. Cohen, 'Baseball as a National Religion', in L. Schneider, ed., *Religion, Culture and Society* (New York, Wiley, 1964), p. 37.
28 S. Edgell and D. Jary, 'Football: A Sociological Eulogy', in Smith *et al.*, eds, *op. cit.*
29 S. B. Linder, *The Harried Leisure Class* (New York, Columbia University Press, 1970), pp. 107–9.
30 N. Elias and E. Dunning, 'Folk Football in Medieval and Early Modern Britain', in E. Dunning, ed., *The Sociology of Sport* (London, Cass, 1971), p. 122.
31 W. W. Schroeder and V. Obenhaus, *Religion in American Culture* (New York, Free Press, 1964), pp. 43–4.
32 M. F. Nimkoff, *Marriage and the Family* (Boston, Houghton Mifflin, 1947), pp. 227–8.
33 Anderson, *op. cit.*, p. 122.
34 S. Vatuk, *Kinship and Urbanization* (Berkeley, University of California Press, 1972), p. 178.
35 J. Tusquets, 'The Political Significance of British and Spanish National Games', *Comparative Education*, No. 2, 1969.
36 W. Pickering, 'Religion: A Leisure Time Pursuit', in D. A. Martin, ed., *A Sociological Yearbook of Religion in Britain* (London, SCM Press, 1968).

37   A. Touraine, *The Post-Industrial Society* (London, Wildwood House, 1974), p. 214.
38   O. E. Klapp, *Collective Search for Identity* (New York, Holt, Rinehart, 1964), p. 139.

PART THREE LEISURE PLANNING AND POLICIES

Chapter 9

Consumers and Demand

In this chapter we shall consider in some detail one side of the 'planning and policies' equation: that of the need that people have for leisure and recreation, and we shall leave until the next chapter the 'supply' side of the equation (though at some points the two aspects come together). We shall first examine such economic factors in leisure as aggregate expenditures, trends and forecasts of trends, and the nature of the leisure market. A major variable in demand is time available for leisure: at the end of the day, week, year and lifetime. Socio-economic and other characteristics also influence the level and type of demand. Many leisure activities make demands on land and water space and the growth of some sports is limited by the amount of natural resources available. We shall consider the amount and types of activity in three particular spheres of leisure: sport, the arts and holidays. Finally, we shall briefly examine the role played by the mass media of communication in influencing the level of demand for leisure activities.

The economics of leisure

A good deal of leisure is virtually unaffected by economic considerations. Pleasurable social contact, physical recreation which involves no resources or equipment, relaxing or pottering about, are types of 'informal' leisure which present no planning problems. Much leisure activity, however, involves using goods or services which have to be provided by public or private enterprise. This type of leisure is 'demanded' and 'consumed' in the same way as the products and services of other industries.

It is extremely difficult to make even an estimate of how much money is spent annually on all forms of leisure. Official British statistics on consumers' expenditure list two categories which unambiguously refer to leisure – 'miscellaneous recreational goods' and 'entertainment and recreational services' – but in 1973 these accounted for only 2·3 per cent and 1·9 per cent respectively of the total national expenditure.[1] However, a number of other items of personal expenditure (apart from expenditure for business purposes) may be attributable to leisure, and these are set out, for 1963 and 1973, in Table 2. The general conclusion is that, during the most recent ten years for which figures were available at the time of writing, expenditure on leisure as a proportion of total expenditure rose only very slightly. Furthermore, we can pinpoint the major source of this increase: in 1963 expenditure on the purchase and running of motor vehicles was 6·3 per cent of all expenditure; in 1973 it rose to 9·2 per cent. The *Leisure Industries Review, 1973–74*, using a different definition of leisure categories and a different basis of calculating leisure expenditure, notes that 'an increasing proportion of the household budget is now being spent on leisure and other discretionary goods and services'.[2]

Table 2   *Consumers' expenditure on leisure (at current prices)*

	As % of total national consumers' expenditure	
	1963	1973
Miscellaneous recreational goods[a]	2·0	2·3
Entertainment and recreational services[a]	1·7	1·9
Alcohol[b]	3·1	3·9
Tobacco[b]	4·1	2·9
Motor vehicles[b]	6·3	9·2
Books, newspapers, magazines and periodicals[b]	1·1	1·2
Travel[b]	2·3	2·0
	20·6	23·4
Total national consumers' expenditure	£20,118m	£44,855m

[a]Source: *National Income and Expenditure, 1974*.
[b]Source: *Family Expenditure Survey, 1973*, HMSO, 1974.

So far, the analysis has been in terms of *proportions* of all expenditure devoted to leisure. But we must not overlook the increase in the absolute amount of total consumers' expenditure, of which leisure has had slightly more than its fair share. In 1963 consumers' expenditure amounted to £27,427m and in 1973 £35,759m, both at 1970 prices. This represents an increase during the ten years of 30 per cent in real purchasing power. It seems reasonable, then, to conclude that leisure spending has increased, but not appreciably more than spending generally. If spending on some leisure pursuits – for example, on bingo and recreational boats – has risen dramatically, this has to some extent been at the expense of other pursuits, notably cinemagoing. A similar pattern seems to be evident in America. According to Fisk, there is no evidence that 'total measured leisure' expenditures are expanding more rapidly than expenditures on all consumer goods in the United States.[3]

Time available for leisure

Although most of us have some time for leisure, the actual amount will depend on the time taken up by work and other obligations. While it is possible for a high level of demand for leisure resources to be generated in a short space of time, it is reasonable to assume that in general the more time we have for leisure the more goods and services we will demand. Changes which have taken place, and are likely to take place, in the average time available for leisure are therefore relevant to an assessment of demand. These changes affect mainly the length of the work week, the work year and the work life.

At the beginning of this century a *normal* working week of 52–4 hours was general among manual workers, reduced after the First World War to 48 hours. There was little change in the 1920s and 1930s, and it was only after the Second World War that a general reduction from 48 to 44 hours took place. By successive small changes the working week of most industrial workers was reduced to 40 hours, which remains the present position. Prior to the Second World War there was little divergence between normal hours and actual hours; overtime was rarely worked. Since then, substantial and persistent overtime has remained a feature of the British industrial scene. As normal working hours have been reduced, there has been a tendency towards a corresponding increase in overtime. While in 1948 actual hours were two hours above normal, in 1972 they were five hours above.[4] Figures for non-manual workers have been collected only recently; there is a broader spread in the range of normal hours worked, but the average is something like 37–8 hours, with little overtime. A small number of firms have introduced flexible working hours. By contrast with the four-day week which operates in a few firms and which allows a block of three days' free time, flexible hours offer greater discretion in arranging the work and leisure day. The long weekend, however, will probably grow in popularity and the 30-hour week, when it comes, is more likely to take the form of a four-day week than a six-hour day.[5]

The chief factors in determining the length of the work year are the duration of public and employment-based annual holidays. It is the latter which have increased most markedly this century. Annual holiday entitlement for manual workers was rare until 1919, but started to grow in the 1920s and 1930s. By 1938 nearly half the labour force had paid holiday entitlements – mostly one week for manual workers and 2–3 weeks for non-manual workers. By 1955 nearly all manual workers had achieved two weeks, and by 1972 many had achieved three weeks. While accurate figures are difficult to obtain, it is known that trade unions have recently achieved a fourth week of annual holiday for several million workers. It is estimated that more than a third of all non-manual workers now have over four weeks holiday entitlement. As for the future, one somewhat optimistic forecast is that by the year 2001 62 per cent of the population will have at least four weeks, and 38 per cent at least six weeks.[6]

The length of work life is determined by the age of entering and leaving the labour force and (in the case of women) the length of any break in work life due to having and bringing up children. In recent years two trends have combined to shorten the average work life: young people have tended to remain longer in full-time education, and the retirement age has been lowered. For women, however, the length of work life has probably been increasing slightly, because of more stable employment opportunities for them and a more permanent pattern of married women working. Each of these trends is likely to continue. On the one hand, extended full-time education and early retirement will result in a shortening of work life, while on the other hand more married women working on a fairly permanent basis will lengthen the average work life.

To sum up the present and probable future trends in time available for leisure: (1) in recent years actual weekly hours have shown only a very small rate of decline, and there is no reason to expect a rapid change, (2) the length of work life has been gradually decreasing for men but not for women, again with little prospect of more rapid reduction, (3) the biggest change has been, and probably will be, in the increase in annual paid holiday entitlement. If there is such a thing as a 'leisure revolution', it is in the growing number of people able to take holidays away from home for longer periods, including holidays abroad.

Factors affecting demand

Demand for different types of leisure and recreation experience is impossible to measure directly, since present rates of activity reflect not only demand but also supply.[7] It is often only after a certain kind of leisure facility or experience is made available that people become aware that they 'need' it. Many factors affect the level and type of demand, and of these we shall consider eight of the more important influences: time available, money available in relation to cost, occupation or class position, level of education, car ownership, stage in the life-cycle, demographic and geographical factors, and traditional and current attitudes.

In the previous section we considered the trends in time available for leisure. The increasing length of paid holiday entitlement conceded by employers has led to a growth in the holiday industry. Shorter periods of available leisure time range from the evening, half day and whole day to the weekend, including the long weekend which merges into the short holiday. The length of each period of time available is important in allowing or restricting the choice of what to do and where to go. Some leisure activities need a relatively long uninterrupted period of time if they are to be engaged in or enjoyed to the full. For short periods of free time, proximity of the resource or facility – in the home or only a short distance from it – is a vital factor in demand.

Cost, whether of the use of facilities, travel to them or equipment for them, is another factor. The BTA–Keele National Recreation Survey showed, not unexpectedly, that in almost every pursuit participation increases with income.[8] But it is difficult to disentangle the effects of income from those of social class, education, etc. and there is not always a correlation between low income and cheap pursuits or between high income and more expensive pursuits. Swimming and hiking, for example, are cheap pastimes which are relatively unpopular among the lower income groups and popular among the better-off. But some expensive pursuits like golf *are* virtually restricted to the middle- and higher-income groups.

Class position, usually measured in terms of broad occupational groups, has a marked influence on participation in active leisure pursuits. In the survey quoted above, it was found that higher-status occupational groups had a much wider recreational experience than others: 10 per cent of manual workers, but only 2 per cent of executives, had never taken part in any of a long list of activities. From their smaller survey in the London region, Young and Willmott calculated that professional and managerial men averaged 18·3 leisure activities at least once during the year, compared with 12·1 for semi-skilled and unskilled men.[9] If, as the evidence cited in Chapter 5 appears to suggest, there is a relationship between type of work and preferred ways of spending leisure, then any change in occupational distribution may be expected to have an effect on the type of demand for leisure goods and services.

A further factor influencing demand for leisure is education. The ever-broadening curriculum in formal and further education is introducing both young and older people to an increasing range of interests and activities.[10] School experience includes musical, dramatic, artistic and physical pursuits, and through this experience the basis for subsequent demand is laid. The opportunity exists for a choice, limited only by the individual's own knowledge and the facilities available, to be made in the kind of leisure activities he wishes to pursue. In adult life the various 'taste publics' are clearly the result of educational among other influences, though the independent effect of educational level is not easy to disentangle from that of other advantages which education may bring, such as higher income and socio-economic position.

Use of a car has been found to have a pervasive effect on leisure activities. More vividly and tangibly than most other determinants of recreation demand, car ownership has revolutionised people's use of leisure time.[11] Car ownership has the effect of increasing participation in leisure pursuits as a whole and in certain activities in particular. Between 1960 and 1965 car-owning households had more than twice the non-car-owning rate of participation in swimming, tennis, golf and camping, but there was much less difference between the two groups in playing team games, bowls and fishing.[12] Furthermore, research has shown that working-class car owners are like people with cars in other classes in the frequency, for example, of their playing sports and eating meals outside their home.[13]

Another very important consideration is stage in the life-cycle. Choice of leisure activities, and rates of participation in them, are different for young single men and women, married couples without children, then with children, after the children leave home, and in the period of retirement. The Government Social Survey national enquiry highlighted the sharp break in sports participation which occurs with marriage and before the arrival of children.[14] This applies especially to women but also to men. There is sometimes a return to active recreation when the family has been reared. The relative importance of leisure in the family's set of priorities at different stages is also significant.[15] Young couples saving hard for a home of their own are likely to devote little of their income to leisure. With small children they will tend to spend more time and money in and around the home. Consequently it may be only when they approach middle age that couples may have the resources to take up new or resume old leisure activities if they wish. Single people will, however, not have been subject to such limitations on their demand for leisure pursuits.

It is fairly obvious that demographic and geographical factors will have an influence on the level and type of demand for leisure facilities in any one community. Population size and growth rate, regional variations and migration movements may also produce marked differences in the total pattern of leisure demand. Sufficiently populated 'catchment areas' are necessary to justify the provision of costly amenities such as indoor sports or leisure centres. People in sparsely populated areas are therefore likely to have to travel considerable distances to get access to such facilities, which may mean that in such areas effective demand is very small or even nil. Something similar may be said of people who live at a considerable distance from natural amenities (and their associated leisure activities) such as mountains or the sea, although day trips or longer visits to distant amenities are not ruled out.

A final factor in demand which deserves brief mention is that of local or societal traditional attitudes towards leisure and recreation provision. The strength of following for forms of folk-dancing, choral groups, the various codes of football, opera or wrestling varies greatly between, say, the North East, the North West and South Wales, and may reach down to quite local district differences.[16] Traditional and current attitudes may affect the level of public support to establish leisure facilities of different kinds; thus recreational provision may be motivated by arguments favouring physical fitness, the avoidance of delinquency, developing character, and so on. Or opinion – and hence demand – may be persuaded by concepts of improved community provision, social welfare and the general quality of life.

Such concepts as leisure 'facilities' and 'provision', together with the fact that we have national sports and arts councils, may lead to the impression that the major components of demand are sport and leisure. This is not the case, since surveys of how people actually spend their time show the prime importance of out-of-home social activities and entertainment. A survey of outdoor leisure activities in the Northern Region revealed that visiting friends, pubs or clubs, and going to places of entertainment or to church accounted for 65 per cent of all reported activities on an average Saturday and for 57 per cent on an average Sunday.[17] A survey in London came to a similar conclusion: 'it seems that out-of-home social activities (eating/drinking/club visiting), entertainments (theatre/cinema) and sightseeing and pleasure trips (visiting the seaside/parks/countryside) are the most popular recreation activities of Londoners'.[18]

Demands on space

Having looked at the amount of time available and other factors which affect the demand for leisure facilities in general, we may now turn to another important dimension – that of space. In this section we shall consider some non-sport leisure demands on open space, leaving sport for separate treatment in the next section.

For men, gardening is the second most popular leisure pursuit after television viewing, occupying on average some 12 per cent of leisure time and rising to 22 per cent on summer weekdays.[19] For women, gardening is surpassed in popularity only by television, crafts and hobbies, reading and general social activities. About 14m out of the 18m homes in Britain have some kind of garden, and it has been estimated that land devoted to gardens covers an estimated 620,000 acres (about the area of Dorset). Gardening is more popular among professional and managerial employees than among semi-skilled and unskilled. Assuming that the future social structure will contain more people in the higher socio-economic groups, a slight rise in gardening activity is forecast to the end of the century.[20] At least, a rise in the *demand* for gardens may be forecast – whether that demand is satisfied will depend on the amount of land available for that purpose.

The demand for parks and playgrounds also presents problems of land usage. Although parks in inner urban areas are sometimes thought to have outlived their usefulness, a survey of visitors to parks in inner London in 1964 showed that 70 per cent of the population aged fifteen and over had visited at least one open space in the month prior to interview, and 39 per cent had done so in the previous week.[21] Teenagers and people with dogs made an above-average number of visits, as did those living in areas exceptionally well provided with open space (proximity to a park is obviously important). The pattern of park usage by visitors from home shows morning, afternoon and evening peaks, while visits made from workplaces show peaks in the lunch break and immediately after work.

Three other non-sport demands on open space may be briefly mentioned. A British Tourist Authority survey showed that in 1970 over 1m households and 3m individuals took part in mobile caravanning or camping.[22] Since these are activities favoured by better-off people, increasing demand for them may be expected. The public use of common land was the subject of another national survey, which concluded that many commons are visited by the public only occasionally, and that most public use occurs on a few particularly attractive and conveniently situated commons.[23] Finally, data collected by the British Waterways Board show that the leisure use of canals is on the increase: in 1967 only 6,747 leisure craft were counted on the canals, compared with 14,557 in 1974.[24]

Sport

Many forms of sport require the use of land or water space. Data on rates of participation are available from the two national surveys carried out in recent years, but it is important to recognise that regular active participants in even the most popular activities represent a small proportion of the total population. The *Planning for Leisure* survey, involving interviews with nearly 6,000 individuals, found that swimming in pools (indoor and outdoor) and dancing were the two most popular activities in 1965–6. About 17 per cent of men and 9 per cent of women went swimming regularly, and 12 per cent of men and 13 per cent of women went dancing regularly.[25] Table tennis and soccer were the next two most popular activities, with participation rates of 8–11 per cent.

Considerable variation in participation rates in the various sports was found between 'domestic age' and socio-economic categories. For single males aged 15–18 swimming and soccer were the most popular activities, changing to dancing and ten-pin bowls (the latter having probably declined since the survey took place) for the single 19–22 group, reverting to swimming for the married 23–45 group, to dancing for the 46–60s, and bowls for the over-60s.[26] For women, there was less change, dancing and swimming being popular in all domestic age groups. Among socio-economic groups golf was the most popular sport for employers, managers and professionals but low down the list for manual and junior non-manual employees. Soccer was popular among the latter groups, but rare among the employers, managers and professionals.

Apart from active participation, substantial numbers of people attend various sports and games as spectators. In the survey quoted above, soccer and cricket attracted up to 27 per cent and 14 per cent respectively of regular male spectators. Only at swimming galas was attendance by women greater than that by men, and there were some significant differences among domestic age and socio-economic groups.

The other national survey (BTA–Keele) gives information about the sporting activities of a sample of 3,000 individuals, but the questions asked were quite different and the two sets of results are difficult to compare. The two surveys agree that swimming is the single most popular sport, but the BTA–Keele survey excludes dancing and table tennis as sports, and gives a much lower figure (4 per cent) for experiencing any kind of team game in 1965. Although the measures of demand for particular sports differ between the two surveys (and hence give different rank orders of participation rates), it is common ground that possession of a car, higher income and socio-economic status are all associated with higher participation rates, especially in the extensive resource-using sports such as golf and sailing.

The assessment of present demand for sport amenities is of less practical importance than the prediction of future demand. In many cases there are no past data with which to compare recent survey results, and so it has not been possible to use techniques normally employed for short-term forecasting. In this context, the method used by NOP Market Research Ltd to forecast rates of leisure activity in the Northern Region[27] and of angling on a national scale in 1980[28] are particularly interesting. The survey data for particular leisure activities were related to eleven demographic characteristics of participants for which 1980 forecasts were available (e.g. age, sex, car ownership). The activities expected to increase most sharply in popularity were golf, camping and caravanning, motor cycle/car racing/rallying, and trips to the country.

The arts

Any discussion of 'the arts' is bedevilled by the vagueness of the term, and clarity of thought is not made any easier by value-laden categories such as 'popular arts', 'fine arts', and so on. Furthermore, data on demand for various forms of the arts are much scarcer than for sports. Without attempting the difficult task of compiling figures for 'interest' or 'activity' in the many different arts, we may seek to reach some broad conclusions about the scale of current demand in five relevant spheres: drama; music, opera and ballet; films; visual arts; and literature and libraries.

Drama includes the professional theatre, the amateur theatre, and theatre for young people (mainly amateur but with some professional companies). Although the word 'drama' is often attached to certain types of film and television programme, it seems better to leave this for separate consideration under the mass media (below). In 1973 there were an estimated 276 theatres in professional use throughout the country.[29] In addition, there are theatres for educational, cultural or youth use and theatres for amateur groups. The Arts Council estimates that attendance at performances given by subsidised theatre companies amounts to over 5m a year and annual audiences for young people's theatre performances are about 3m. Two items of information which appear to be lacking are the total number of annual attendances at professional theatres, and the extent of multiple attendances by regular theatregoers. Some information about the relative proportions of performers and spectators would also be worth having.

Music, opera and ballet are similarly short of statistics, except a few concerning professional standards. Thus it is known that over 208,000 children and other students take the examinations of the Associated Board of the Royal Schools of Music each year. Apart from musical performances in concert halls, there are substantial, but precisely unknown, attendances at open-air concerts in many cities, including both lunchtime and evening performances.

More is known about the audiences for films in cinemas, which have over the last quarter-century literally been decimated: in 1946 there were 1,635m cinema attendances, compared with 163m in 1972. To some extent, this reduction has been compensated for by the showing of films on television.

The visual arts may be taken to include, on the 'performing' side, such activities as painting and sculpting (the Central Office of Information handbook quoted above also includes architecture, but this appears to be more a work than a leisure art). On the spectating side, there are museums and art galleries, though no doubt much visiting of such places is combined with an active interest in the particular art. A recent survey of visitors to three London museums, although not designed to obtain total attendance figures, revealed that visitors had received far more formal education than the general population, though proximity to a museum was a most important factor influencing visits.[30]

Finally, there is the leisure component in literature and libraries. Provided one does not use too narrow a definition of 'the arts', here is more than a quantitative match for the most popular sport. The figures of expenditure on books, etc. given earlier in this chapter generally underestimate the proportion of the population and the amount of time involved. To take one simple statistic, about one-third of the total population are members of public libraries.[31] There is undoubtedly a greater demand for escapist novels and other 'light' reading than for more 'serious' books, but a glance at the bestseller lists shows that the latter category is by no means confined to a small minority of readers.

Holidays

A good deal of information has been collected about the popularity of various forms of holiday. Although, as we saw in an earlier section, more people have obtained longer holiday entitlements, this has not resulted in a dramatic increase in the number of holidays taken. Between 1964 and 1972 there was only a 21 per cent increase in the total number of holidays and in only one case (1969–70) was there an increase of more than 5 per cent on the previous year.[32] During this period the domestic holiday market was relatively stable, but the number of overseas holidays taken by British residents rose by 76 per cent, while the number of visits from overseas increased by 150 per cent. Also, the modest increase in domestic holidays was concentrated in the taking of additional rather than main holidays.

Except for the elderly and the lowest income groups, who take fewer holidays, the characteristics of holidaymakers mostly correspond to those of the general population. For additional holidays, however, the higher socio-economic groups predominate. Newman has calculated that in 1970 14 per cent of the highest (AB) socio-economic group took 56 per cent of the second or subsequent holidays.[33] Holidaymakers going abroad tend to have both higher incomes and freedom from family ties. Newman also suggested that different social class groups tend to seek different types of holiday experience according to their views of the social world. At one extreme is the passive, collective and highly organised holiday camp, and at the other the active, privatised and little-organised motorised caravan or camping holiday.

The type of accommodation sought by holidaymakers is an important feature of demand. Although the proportion of holidays spent with relatives or friends has declined in recent years, this remains the single most popular type of accommodation. Over the last two decades the larger hotels have just about retained their share, but there has been a relative decline in holidays spent in boarding houses and unlicensed hotels.[34] The major increase has been in the more informal type of accommodation: rented flats, houses and cottages, camping, and above all caravans. In 1972 tents and caravans provided accommodation for 25 per cent of all main holidays, compared with 17 per cent in 1965.

The preferred geographical location of holidays has been subject to fluctuation over time. The South West is by far the most important holiday region and has increased its share from 16 per cent in 1960 to 22 per cent in 1970. Other regions, notably the South East and the North/North East, have taken a lower share. The measure of concentration of holidaymaking, previously weak, has increased, while the ties between industrial regions and specific holiday resorts have been reduced.[35] The car has encouraged the development of small resort villages and caravan sites located away from existing resorts, and the process of dispersal has been aided by the rising costs of the traditional holiday. But the lure of the coast is still paramount: about 75 per cent of all main holidays in Britain include a stay by the seaside.

The holiday season is crowded into a very brief period, influenced chiefly by the timing of school holidays. In 1971, 64 per cent of all main holidays were taken in July and August, though additional holidays were more evenly spread throughout the year, the single most important month being September.[36] Over the past decade there has been very little change in the timing of holidays.

Finally, there is the question of the pattern of future demand for holidays. There seems to be some scope for a continued increase in the taking of second holidays, which should help to even out the demand for holiday accommodation and facilities over more of the year (though, in the absence of a staggering of school holidays, the trend may not have much further to go). Young and Willmott found that between half and two-thirds of the people in their survey expressed a preference to take more leisure as annual holiday rather than as a daily or weekly reduction of hours worked.[37] So total demand for holidays is likely to increase, though the economic climate and the comparative value offered by the various branches of the holiday industry will help to determine which type of holiday will meet with the most demand.

The role of the mass media

There is no doubt that the mass media of communication constitute the biggest single influence on demand for a wide variety of leisure activities and interests. Evidence, derived primarily from continuous monitoring surveys, suggests that television, radio and newspapers account for about thirty hours a week of the average British adult's time.[38] It is estimated that over 90 per cent of all households own or rent at least one television set. The consequence for leisure is that television is not only the medium through which very large numbers of people gain particular experiences, vicarious though these may be – television, by portraying both leisure activities and interests and the enthusiasts who demonstrate and talk about them, encourages others to take part in them personally. The media are thus both a leisure interest in themselves and also a catalyst for other interests.

Studies have been made of the effects of the growth in popularity of television on other leisure pursuits. It has led to a decline in cinema attendances, theatre-going, radio-listening, and in the reading of fiction.[39] But the breadth of people's leisure interests does not seem to have narrowed to any appreciable extent, and activities such as reading serious books, gardening, watching and playing sports, and attending clubs have suffered little or no decline in popularity. There is also some historical evidence that as new passive types of recreation have become available they have replaced mainly other equally passive pursuits.[40]

The growth of the mass media poses the question of the *quality* of demand for leisure in perhaps its most acute form. Indeed, those who use the concept of 'demand' tend to beg one of the most important questions in this field: should society simply respond to people's expressed or 'economic' demand for particular types of leisure experience? Or should society be concerned with shaping demand through educational and other influences in accordance with values concerning what is thought to be 'good' leisure? The possible answers to these and related questions will become clearer when we consider in the next chapter the supply side of leisure.

REFERENCES

1   *National Income and Expenditure* (London, HMSO, 1974).
2   *Leisure Industries Review, 1973–74* (Epping, Gower Economic Publications, 1973), p. xv.
3   G. Fisk, *Leisure Spending Behaviour* (Philadelphia, University of Pennsylvania Press, 1963), p. 29.
4   *Department of Employment Gazette*.
5   P. Willmott, 'Some Social Trends', *Urban Studies*, November 1969.
6   M. Young and P. Willmott, *The Symmetrical Family* (London, Routledge, 1973), p. 131.
7   I. Cosgrove and R. Jackson, *The Geography of Recreation and Leisure* (London, Hutchinson, 1972), p. 95.
8   British Travel Association–University of Keele, *Pilot National Recreation Survey*, 1967.
9   Young and Willmott, *op. cit.*, p. 219.
10 D. Molyneux, 'A Framework for Recreation Research', in T. L. Burton, ed., *Recreation Research and Planning* (London, George Allen & Unwin, 1970), p. 50.
11 *Ibid.*, p. 51.
12 J. A. Patmore, *Land and Leisure* (Harmondsworth, Penguin, 1972), p. 38.
13 Young and Willmott, *op. cit.*, p. 224.
14 K. K. Sillitoe, *Planning for Leisure* (London, HMSO, 1969).
15 S. R. Parker, 'Professional Life and Leisure', *New Society*, 9 October 1974.
16 Molyneux, *op. cit.*, pp. 52–3.
17 North Regional Planning Committee, *Outdoor Leisure Activities in the Northern Region* (National Opinion Polls, 1969).
18 S. Law, *Greater London Recreation Study: Report of Initial Results* (GLC Department of Planning and Transportation, 1974).
19 Patmore, *op. cit.*, p. 36.
20 Young and Willmott, *op. cit.*, p. 371.
21 Greater London Council Planning Department, 'Surveys of the Use of Open Space', 1968.
22 British Tourist Authority, *Survey of Mobile Caravanning and Camping* (London, Countryside Commission, 1970).
23 J. F. Wager, 'Outdoor Recreation on Common Land', *Journal of the Town Planning Institute*, November 1967.
24 British Waterways Board, *Recreational Use of Inland Waterways, Data 1967–1974*.
25 Sillitoe, *op. cit.*, p. 119.
26 *Ibid.*, p. 122.
27 North Regional Planning Committee, *op. cit.*
28 National Opinion Polls, *National Angling Survey*, 1971.
29 Central Office of Information, *The Promotion of the Arts in Britain* (London, 1973), p. 6.
30 P. Wingfield-Digby, *Visitors to Three London Museums* (London, HMSO, 1974), p. viii.
31 Central Office of Information, *op. cit.*, p. 27.
32 British Tourist Authority, *The British on Holiday*, 1973. A 'holiday' is defined as four or more nights away from home.
33 B. Newman, 'Holidays and Social Class', in M. A. Smith *et al.*, eds, *Leisure and Society in Britain* (London, Allen Lane, 1973), p. 235.

34 Patmore, *op. cit.*, p. 144.
35 Cosgrove and Jackson, *op. cit.*, p. 117.
36 *Leisure Industries Review, op. cit.*, p. 61.
37 Young and Willmott, *op. cit.*, p. 142.
38 Sources quoted in J. Curran and J. Tunstall, 'Mass Media and Leisure', in Smith *et al.*, eds, *op. cit.*, p. 212.
39 W. A. Belson, *The Impact of Television* (London, Crosby Lockwood, 1967).
40 K. Roberts, *Leisure* (London, Longman, 1970), p. 74.

Chapter 10

Providers and Provision

Having considered in the previous chapter the nature of demand for leisure, we shall now turn to the various means by which this demand may be met. We shall first review the aims of planning in the leisure sphere, paying particular attention to the sometimes competing claims of control and choice. Then we shall briefly describe the activities and values of some of the chief public and private providers of different kinds of leisure facilities. The problems of land availability and leisure traffic are the main concerns under the heading of 'spatial imbalances'. Scarcity of natural resources leads to the need to reconcile conflicting interests and to conserve such resources when threatened by over-use. Finally, there are various levels of supply – national, regional, local – which meet different levels of need and often have a big influence in shaping demand.

The aims of planning

Planning, in its broadest sense, ultimately determines the range of leisure opportunities – that is, the types of leisure environments – available to the people of urban-industrial societies. Burton has summed up the aims of planning as preventing the undesirable effects of development while promoting the desirable ones.[1] But if leisure is to mean free choice of activities, there are special problems connected with the planning process. If the defining characteristic of leisure is that it encourages and promotes opportunities for the exercise of choice, it follows that the purpose in planning for leisure is to provide the maximum possible diversity. Planning must recognise the existence of a multiplicity of individual and societal goals. Far from being unitary in purpose, the aims of planning must be pluralist: to provide a wide range of leisure opportunities so as to offer a wide range of choices.

Before starting a summary review of the bodies responsible for leisure provision, we need to recognise a further conceptual and value problem. 'Planning for leisure' is really a misnomer, though 'planning for recreation' is an achievable and (depending on the values of the planners) probably desirable goal. This distinction becomes clearer if we accept the somewhat unusual but perceptive definition of 'recreation' offered by Herbert Gans: the artifacts, facilities and institutions which people employ for leisure behaviour.[2] Leisure behaviour is subjective, and is satisfying and desirable to the extent that it is freely chosen. Governmental and commercial agencies can and should plan recreation facilities with the intent and hope that they will be attractive enough for people to use in leisure behaviour. The means can be socially provided, but not the end, which is the sphere of individual choice and experience. There is a close parallel here with education, which can legitimately teach people how to think but not what to think. Planning can enable people to derive chosen leisure experiences from their environment, but it cannot legitimately decide for them what leisure they should have.

Public enterprise

Various leisure amenities are provided or financed by public bodies at national, regional and local level. It will be convenient to consider such amenities separately for sports, the arts, and other leisure.

In 1965 an advisory Sports Council was established, followed by the various regional Sports Councils in 1966. In 1972 the Sports Council was given executive powers under the Minister with special responsibility for sport, and in 1974 the Minister's remit was extended to 'recreation'. The government, without being directly involved in promoting sporting activities, provides financial help through the councils to assist organisations responsible for individual sports, to establish sports centres and other recreational facilities, to promote training and coaching facilities, and to assist British teams in international competitions.[3] In 1972–3 the capital investment on facilities for sport and physical recreation of local authorities was £43m, of educational bodies £22m, and of the Sports Councils in England, Wales and Scotland £2½m, but in addition the Sports Councils received £2½m for other expenditure. The central and regional Sports Councils work in close conjunction with the Central Council for Physical Recreation, the National Playing Fields Association and the British Olympic Association. Soon after their inception the regional Sports Councils initiated 'initial appraisals' of such capital-intensive facilities as swimming pools, indoor sports centres, golf courses, etc. Though these appraisals have enabled useful comparisons of provision to be made within regions, they have been criticised for failing to standardise terms of reference and basic definitions.[4]

The law requires all publicly maintained schools in Britain to provide for the physical education (gymnastics, games, athletics, dancing and swimming) of their pupils. In increasing numbers of areas physical education facilities in schools have been expanded to meet the recreational needs of the whole community. Local authorities are the main providers of land and large-scale facilities to be used by the community for recreation – they establish, for instance, playing fields, gymnasia, tennis courts, golf courses, boating lakes, swimming baths and sports centres. At the beginning of 1970 there were 27 sports centres open in England. By March 1974 this had grown rapidly to 167, with 119 under construction and 154 firmly committed, that is, 56 per cent of the 1981 'target' of 779 centres.[5] A good number of these new centres resulted from a policy of joint provision by educational and local authorities. The main advantages claimed for sports centres are that they can cater for as many as twenty different sports under the same roof, and that they can provide for the needs of whole families and can help restore community spirit. But the centres have also been criticised as being too big and impersonal.

The chief organisation promoting the arts dimension of leisure is the Arts Council of Great Britain, which was established in 1946. Its main objects are to develop and improve the knowledge, understanding and practice of the arts, to increase the accessibility of the arts to the public, and to advise and co-operate with government departments, local authorities and other organisations.[6] The council promotes music and drama through grants to professional orchestras, opera, ballet and drama companies, and arranges art exhibitions. Assistance for particular projects is given to individual artists, including painters, sculptors, writers and composers. In 1959 the Arts Council published a survey of existing facilities in London and the provinces,[7] and in the 1960s a slow process of decentralisation via the regional arts associations made more accessible a wide range of activities which had previously been concentrated in and around London. Government aid to the arts also goes directly to certain national libraries, museums and art galleries, the British Film Institute, and other agencies. Nobody knows how much of the £3,000m a year spent on education is devoted to art, music, drama and literature in general and specialist education.[8] All local authorities own and operate public libraries, and many provide theatres, concert halls, museums and art galleries in their areas and support local arts councils and encourage amateur music, drama and arts groups.

Aside from sports and arts, various other leisure activities are catered for or helped by public or voluntary non-profit-making bodies. The following are some examples, not to be taken as an exhaustive list either of activities or of organisations. As a development of the earlier National Parks Commission, the Countryside

Commission was set up in 1968 'to make new provision for the enjoyment of the countryside . . . both to meet public demand and to relieve pressure on remote or outstandingly beautiful places'.[9] The National Trust, a much older voluntary body, came into existence with the major purpose of conserving natural resources for leisure, though the Trust has been criticised for not making its properties freely available to the general public.[10]

In 1919 the Forestry Commission was created, chiefly to secure an adequate stock of timber in case of national emergency. From the 1930s onwards Forest Parks were opened, with camp sites and ready access to upland areas. In recent years the Forestry Commission's policy has been increasingly concerned with the recreational use of woodland, and with visual amenity in particular. The Nature Conservancy, originally set up in 1949 and now part of the Natural Environment Research Council, has a similar policy of making nature reserves accessible for the use and enjoyment of visitors, provided that this does not interfere with the aims of conservation (see below).

An example of public control in a different sphere is the British Broadcasting Corporation which, through its radio and television programmes, plays a major role (relatively recently in competition with commercial organisations) in our leisure and which has probably done more to make music and drama available to a mass audience than any other single agency. Finally, a number of non-commercial organisations cater for the leisure needs of particular sections of the population: thus it has been estimated that 29 per cent of young people have had some connection with the youth service (mainly as youth club members),[11] while some leisure amenities for the aged are provided by such bodies as Old People's Welfare Committees.

An important consideration in leisure provision by public enterprise is the values of the planners and providers. It is inevitable that these values will have some influence on the range of leisure opportunities that exist in any community or society. Unlike private enterprise, which provides according to market demand helped along by advertising, public enterprise relies on the planners and providers knowing (or believing they know) what people want. That is why it is important that responsibilities for identifying leisure needs and providing opportunities to meet them should be spread widely.[12] But, as Isabel Emmett points out, the aim of suppliers is seldom the democratic one of finding out what people say they want to do, and then providing facilities for them to do it – the aim is more likely to be paternalist (though often in heavy disguise): persuading them to do what is 'good for them' in the view of the suppliers.[13] The imposition of 'alien' values is a particularly controversial issue with regard to the new towns. Thus William Bacon has strongly criticised the middle-class planning and 'caretaking' process which, he claims, is based on radically different values and social experiences from those of the working-class people it is supposed to serve and is unresponsive to their culture.[14]

Since the sphere of public provision cannot rely on economic market forces to decide what leisure goods and services to supply, it must be guided either by knowledge of what people want or by what is in effect a system of public patronage. The concept of patronage originally applied to private citizens or groups supporting the work of artists, but today it is more evident in the activities of government bodies, the Arts Council, the BBC and so on in catering for minority tastes. Which tastes are catered for, and the ways in which they are catered for, depend on how articulate and well-organised the representatives of various tastes are, how skilful they are at inducing the wider public to acquiesce in their views, and how effective they are at bringing pressure on patronage-dispensing bodies. Official patronage can be criticised on grounds of paternalism, for it could be argued that people ought to be allowed individually to decide which leisure interests should receive their support, instead of having this decision taken for them by public authorities. Against this, it is pointed out that traditional live arts such as opera, ballet and the performance of classical music would have the greatest difficulty in surviving without some form of patronage.[15] In urban areas, sports requiring open spaces would become prohibitively expensive because of the high cost of land.

Private enterprise

In the previous section we took a rather wide view of public enterprise to include, besides government bodies at different levels, voluntary non-profit-making organisations. The private sphere of leisure provision is similarly mixed, including those commercial enterprises which either supply leisure goods and services to the paying public or seek to occupy the leisure of their own employees (sometimes called 'industrial recreation').

It is possible to consider some of the larger public providers of leisure amenities as falling within the 'leisure industries'. But the term is more appropriately used in connection with commercial organisations which exist specifically to cater for people's leisure interests. The leisure industries are essentially a product of the last hundred years, and many of them are of much more recent origin than that. The technology and methods of organisation that have proved effective in the more basic sectors of the economy have been widely adapted to 'sell' leisure.[16] Music, sport and numerous other goods and services used in the pursuit of recreation and amusement are now manufactured and marketed by organisations whose primary aim is to induce consumption of these products. Although commercial suppliers will normally prefer larger to smaller markets for their products, it does not follow that minority interests will be ignored. Provided that meeting minority demands is profitable, entrepreneurs can and do cater for those demands. Some commercial organisations, principally the independent television companies, are responsible to a statutory body that has the power to insist that minority tastes are catered for.

Private ownership of leisure facilities, whether for sport or aesthetic enjoyment, is an important element in provision and public access. Many existing sports grounds are privately owned for the exclusive use of club members or works employees: in Lancashire, for example, 42 per cent of all sports grounds are in private hands.[17] While this implies some restriction on availability, it may not be serious, for many sports naturally develop club structures and have an important social element. Private ownership of land and buildings usable for leisure purposes may also prohibit public access, though the opening up of stately homes to fee-paying visitors has in recent years become a substantial leisure industry, with visitors to some of the more popular locations running into hundreds of thousands each year. With the increasing popularity of boating and yachting, privately financed marinas have been developed. The most ambitious scheme so far is at Brighton, which, in addition to moorings for 3,000 craft, includes houses and flats, shopping, sports and entertainment facilities and an exhibition centre.[18]

Many indoor leisure activities are provided for by the commercial sector. To mention briefly some of the main ones: pubs are important centres of social life which provide not only alcohol but very often also television and sometimes entertainment such as folk and jazz groups. To cater for the increasing popularity of eating out, restaurants offering national dishes of other countries, particularly Chinese, have opened in large numbers. Clubs for different age and interest groups proliferate throughout Britain and are especially noticeable in the north of England. It has been estimated that four out of five people gamble in some way and, with state provision confined to premium bonds, there are many commercial bingo halls, betting shops and gaming clubs. Dancing is provided for by over 3,000 dance halls located throughout Britain. A few of the larger companies engaged in the leisure industries, such as Grand Metropolitan Hotels and Mecca, have interests spread across a number of the above-mentioned and other leisure activities.

One modern version of patronage is sponsorship by private companies, particularly of sports. Because the aim is to advertise products, sponsors favour sporting events that attract the television cameras, notably motor racing, which is estimated to receive 30 per cent of all money given to sport.[19] In 1974 about one in six industrial companies sponsored sport, and in that year they gave about £15m for this purpose.

In view of the volatile market for particular leisure goods and services, some of the larger companies engaged in the leisure business are diversifying their activities in the expectation that they will be able to cash in on the demand for new leisure activities and cut their losses on the old. A spokesman for one of these firms said that earlier they were in the 'entertainment' business but now they regarded themselves as in the 'leisure' business. The significance of this change is that formerly the policy might be summed up as 'getting people into boxes' – cinemas, dance halls, ten-pin bowls, and so on. The current policy is to cater for people's leisure needs in a variety of surroundings – to rely less on captive audiences than on finding out what people want and supplying them with it when and where it is wanted. This would mean the company possibly going into new fields of leisure provision such as sports, travel and hotels.

Spatial imbalances

Land and water resources usable for leisure are not always located where there is most demand for them. Supply is a matter partly of volume but more importantly of location and accessibility. The growth of leisure traffic is a consequent problem of greater access.

The use of land for recreational purposes is long established. It has been estimated that some 3 million acres of rural land in England and Wales (about 8 per cent of the total area) are now in effective recreational use.[20] Since the setting up of the National Parks Commission (later the Countryside Commission) in 1949, ten national parks have been established, powers have been given for designation of areas of outstanding natural beauty, and for the creation of long-distance footpaths. The need for public access to reservoirs has been officially recognised, and some progress has been made in transforming canals into a network of 'cruise-ways'.

Competing claims for land are at the root of the problems that town and country planning tries to solve. Land to which there is access for recreation is rarely reserved for this purpose alone. The problems are made more difficult by the present unequal distribution of recreational land: about 150 acres per 1,000 population in Wales, the West Midlands and the South West, but only 20–30 acres in the East Midlands and the South East.[21] Furthermore, there are no clear criteria for judging the optimum carrying capacity of a particular stretch of land used for recreational purposes. Even more difficult to weigh up are the qualitative merits of different land resources. How does one define 'areas of great landscape value' other than by subjective consensus?

The increasing use of the motor car for leisure purposes has created problems of land use. New roads and motorways have eaten into land previously used for other purposes in both town and country areas. The need to cope with the arrival and parking of vehicles at leisure destinations has also changed – usually for the worse – the character of these destinations. When visitors to the countryside were few, there was room for all – and landowners often turned a blind eye to trespass. But as numbers of pleasure motorists have grown, much of the previous open land has become overrun, many lay-bys have been soiled, much common land has been eroded, and barbed wire and 'keep out' notices bespatter the green belt.[22]

Suggestions have been made for further public regulation and control of road traffic to improve the total situation of leisure provision and access in Britain. Rubinstein and Speakman have spelled out a controversial proposal for motorless zones, a proposal favoured by the Countryside Commission itself.[23] Acts in 1947 and 1968 gave local authorities powers to control traffic in beauty spots, but in practice they usually extend only to restrictions on parking. But a firmer policy of control, to be politically acceptable, would need to be accompanied by better provision for leisure traffic. Restrictions such as segregation of traffic or some form of road pricing would need to be balanced by a greater investment in large-scale road construction to cope with traffic to and from leisure amenities, and perhaps the acceptance of the use of the car at the amenity itself to the extent of building more 'scenic drives' on the North American pattern.

The problem of traffic is part of the larger problem of the use of space in urban areas. The reconstruction of some town centres to meet primarily the demands of commerce and industry for office development encourages only limited daytime use of central areas at the expense of any provision for residential evening, civic or recreational activity.[24] The need is to plan recreational facilities and community amenities in the centre of housing schemes, to make available recreational 'campuses' where all age groups can find some readily accessible opportunity for relaxation and physical recreation. The problems of spatial imbalance are not limited to Britain but are common to most advanced industrial societies. Thus Joffre Dumazedier, writing of conditions in France, deplores the atomism of leisure space, which he attributes to lack of global planning.[25]

Resource scarcity and conservation

Resources used for leisure are both natural and man-made, outdoor and indoor, publicly and privately provided. In this section we shall concentrate on natural, outdoor resources which, by virtue of their finite and sometimes irreplaceable character, involve the need for conservation.

A simple calculation of recreational land available in Britain per head of population might suggest abundance rather than scarcity. The 3 million acres in England and Wales in effective recreational use represent some 65 acres for every 1,000 persons, compared with the National Playing Fields Association recommended standard for urban areas of 6 acres per 1,000 persons of playing space, 1 acre of public open space and 3 acres of school playing fields.[26] But such calculations are misleading: they fail to take into account the varying nature of the land described as in recreational use, its location and the degree of access to it.

Allan Patmore shows in detail that there is a serious imbalance between demand and supply, and that this may lead ultimately to the aesthetic and even physical erosion of resources.[27] He makes a distinction between resource-based and user-oriented land devoted to recreation. With the former it is the quality of the resource irrespective of its location which is important. It may be a unique landscape, crags of high quality for the climber, or the habitat of a rare species of animal or wild flower. Those who wish to visit such places will not be deterred unduly by distance, and the appeal may well be national rather than regional or local.

User-oriented facilities are important more for their location than for their inherent quality. Some sacrifice of quality is accepted, provided that the resource is accessible during the time available: the local canal for an evening's fishing, or a ramble through fields a short way from home. Such resources cater primarily for local needs, their prime market being adjacent urban areas.

With resource-based land serious conflicts often arise between those who seek to enjoy the resource and those concerned, with varying motives, for its preservation. Conservation can take many forms, from absolute preservation of a resource by the rigorous denial of any access or development to a development control in the planning process which accedes only partially to the claims of the conservationists. At one extreme are the nature reserves, where the key to successful conservation may be the almost total exclusion of human access. At the other extreme are the green belts which, though important in active recreational use, have been conceived primarily as a check on urban growth. In between come national parks, areas of outstanding natural beauty and areas of great landscape, historic or scientific value.

The coast is an important resource from a recreational point of view. No part of England and Wales is more than seventy-five miles from tidal water, and one-third of the day trips and three-quarters of all holidays have the seaside as their destination. But there are two different kinds of pressure on the recreational use of the coast. The first is industrial: the expansion of port facilities, the use of estuaries for oil refineries, power stations near the coast, and so on. The second pressure is that which seeks to preserve the coast as far as possible in its natural or semi-natural state. As with inland resources, conservation may conflict with recreation. And, in face of increasing demand for the recreational use of the coast, similar compromises will be necessary. On the one hand, pressures on physical and social capacities push against the limits of beach and sea to absorb varied activities without unacceptable overcrowding. On the other hand, environmental capacity governs the extent to which a coastline can be used before visual deterioration sets in or serious conservation problems arise.

Inland waterways at present face fewer problems of conservation; from a recreational point of view it is more a question of unused potential. Few stretches of inland water and waterways are as fully developed for recreation as they could be.[28] Less than half of the reservoirs are open to leisure use, even for angling, despite growing acceptance in the water-supply profession that such use can be fully compatible with water-purity standards. But there has been some recent development in the recreational use of reservoirs, canals and 'wet' gravel pits.

The hierarchy of supply

Time available for leisure comes in periods of different lengths – the evening, half-day, whole day, weekend and annual holidays. The supply of physical and other facilities needs to be geared to these varying periods, but derives also from the appropriate geographical scale of provision. The conventional scales of such provision are local, regional and national. There are two related assumptions involved in the concept of a hierarchy of supply: (1) the closer a particular leisure facility is, the more people will 'demand' it, and (2) the higher the level of the facility (on a scale roughly from local to national), the more time will people be prepared to spend on travelling to it.[29]

At the local level of provision, the facilities needed are in and around the home and within a short travelling distance of it. Dower has drawn attention to the significance of the home in this respect: 'our homes are the core of our stock of leisure space . . . a developed nation can reasonably expect its housing to be fit also for leisure'.[30] Because of television, the main living-room has gained new importance as a mini-cinema. There must be space elsewhere in the house, however restricted, for the entertainments, hobbies and pastimes of the different family members, including reasonable heating and sound-proofing. Space outside the home is also needed for gardening, parking and tinkering with the car, children's play equipment, and so on.

Beyond the home and garden, but still at a local scale, the needs for leisure provision include indoor and outdoor facilities, those for the different age groups, and for sport, artistic and social purposes. Parks, playing-fields, swimming pools, and hard all-weather surfaces for sports are some of the needs for outdoor provision. Sports halls, multi-purpose leisure centres, arts centres, youth and old-age club premises are among the indoor needs. It is not only a matter of supplying buildings and physical equipment: paid or voluntary staff are needed to man the facilities, to teach, co-ordinate effort, raise funds and help in many other ways.

At the regional scale it is mainly weekend leisure that has to be catered for – amenities which are normally too distant for daily access but perhaps not sufficiently rare or attractive to warrant devoting a holiday to them. Weekend motoring means that the catchment area for outdoor and some indoor amenities is now much wider than hitherto. Sporting activities that require particular locations and informal outdoor leisure are the main outdoor growth areas at regional level. Marinas for weekend sailing enthusiasts, sought-after angling, climbing and skiing locations, country parks and picnic sites are in increasing demand. Some indoor facilities cater for publics including those outside the local area but short of a national scale, and the operational spheres of regional sports and arts councils are evidence of this. The supply of facilities varies not only between but also within regions: thus, for example, there is a 'cultural belt' along the Thames around Maidenhead and Windsor, but a pronounced lack of facilities in the west of the area relative to the east.[31]

Supply at the national scale is concerned mainly with what people do during their holidays, though some 'national' amenities are used on other occasions by people fortunate enough to live near them, and other people may be willing to travel long distances for visits shorter than holidays. Because tourism has major significance for the country's economy, government grants and loans for hotel building have helped to improve the amount of tourist accommodation. Although roads, parks, public monuments, etc. are the responsibility of public authorities to provide or conserve, many other holiday amenities have been commercially provided. In the remoter areas more responsibility rests with public authorities to provide services for both residents and visitors. As Cosgrove and Jackson point out, public supply, up to the present time, has been concentrated in remoter areas, while private supply has prospered close to towns.[32]

It is possible to examine the hierarchy of supply more specifically in respect of particular leisure interests and activities. We shall do this in the next section when relating supply to demand.

The demand–supply relationship

Let us first examine the ways in which different scales of demand for open spaces affect (or at least should affect) the scale of supply.[33] At the most local level the needs of those lacking time, ability or desire to travel far must be met. Small, easily accessible spaces are needed, especially for young children and old people. At the intermediate stage there are more general needs to be satisfied: bigger spaces for the more adventurous play of older children, facilities for such relatively short-period games as tennis or bowls. Such spaces should be within reasonable walking distance of home – up to a mile at most. More specialised demands at the top of the hierarchy are less restricted by time and accessibility. Team games or other sports played for longer periods justify time spent on travel, usually by car or public transport, while parks must be large enough or with adequate amenities to attract families at weekends.

Somewhat parallel considerations apply to the provision of opera to meet various levels of actual and potential demand. There are five permanent, professional opera companies of international standing now in existence – two in London, one in Sussex, and one each in Wales and Scotland (neither with its own opera house).[34] The major gap is thus the North of England's lack of a permanent opera company. There are, however, many small companies either indigenous to or touring in the provinces which provide operatic performances at below international standard. It is sometimes claimed that there is indifference to opera (and to other arts) in the regions but, as Cosgrove and Jackson point out, if there is such indifference then it must reflect the population's long deprivation of facilities. How can anyone be enthusiastic about opera if the nearest permanent company of international standard is 300 miles away?[35]

With most leisure facilities it is true that to a large extent supply creates demand, particularly if the supply is regular and fits in with the life-style of the time and place. Potential demand also depends on the steps which are taken to encourage interest in a particular facility in the schools and via the media. It follows that any assessment of potential demand is made difficult, if not impossible, in a situation of non-provision and lack of knowledge or encouragement to demand provision. Leisure, at least in the forms we have been considering in this and the previous chapter, is not something which human beings need in a basic or 'natural' way. All of us are, in fact, socialised into expressing needs for particular forms of leisure activity, and in the absence of social stimuli we remain oblivious to what could be available to us. A good example of this is the field of artistic expression and appreciation. It has been justifiably claimed that the demand for 'community arts' comes more often from the performers than from the audiences; they create the demand and then satisfy it.[36] But it may be countered that if we were to supply only what had previously been demanded by audiences or other consumers, we would slow down the rate of innovation in society considerably and perhaps stop it altogether. It should be remembered that there was no public clamour for television in the 1930s – it was only when television was provided that the public came to perceive it as a necessary part of life.

Perhaps the key to the link between demand and supply is awareness – on the part of the suppliers of what will 'catch on' and on the part of the spectators or consumers of what is available, or could be made available, for them to demand. As Emmett points out, it is time-consuming and costly for a research unit to find out where a boy living in Oldham can go to learn judo or archery, and it is much more difficult for the boy to find out for himself.[37] The sense of one's own identity in society is even more important: that boy in Oldham will not even *want* to find out about judo or archery if he is led to believe that they are not for people like himself.

REFERENCES

1 T. L. Burton, 'Changing Patterns of Work and Leisure', paper no. 15, Duke of Edinburgh's Study Conference (London, Industrial Society, 1974). See also S. Law, 'Leisure and Recreation: Problems and Prospects', *Planning Outlook* (Newcastle upon Tyne, Summer 1974).
2 H. J. Gans, *People and Plans* (New York, Basic Books, 1968), p. 110.
3 Central Office of Information, *Sport in Britain* (London, 1972), p. 1.
4 J. A. Patmore, *Land and Leisure* (Harmondsworth, Penguin, 1972), p. 58.
5 Sports Council, *Annual Report 1973–74*, p. 20.
6 Central Office of Information, *The Promotion of the Arts in Britain* (London, 1973), p. 2.
7 Arts Council, *Housing the Arts in Great Britain* (London, 1959).
8 A. Dunbar, 'The Arts', in I. Appleton, ed., *Leisure Research and Policy* (Edinburgh, Scottish Academic Press, 1974).
9 'Leisure in the Countryside', Government White Paper, 1966.
10 E. T. Ashton, *People and Leisure* (London, Ginn, 1971), pp. 71–2.
11 J. Leigh, *Young People and Leisure* (London, Routledge, 1971), p. 32.
12 Burton, *op. cit.*
13 I. Emmett, 'Sociological Research in Recreation', in T. L. Burton, ed., *Recreation Research and Planning* (London, George Allen & Unwin, 1970), p. 68.

14 W. Bacon, 'Social Caretaking and Leisure Provision', in S. Parker *et al.*, eds, *Sport and Leisure in Contemporary Society* (Polytechnic of Central London, 1975).

15 K. Roberts, *Leisure* (London, Longman, 1970), p. 81.

16 *Ibid.*, p. 63.

17 Patmore, *op. cit.*, p. 72.

18 A. M. Wren and I. Appleton, 'The Commercial Sector', in I. Appleton, ed., *op. cit.*

19 R. West, 'Sponsored Sports', *New Statesman*, 17 January 1975.

20 *Ibid.*

21 Quoted in I. Cosgrove and R. Jackson, *The Geography of Recreation and Leisure* (London, Hutchinson, 1972), p. 20.

22 M. Dower, 'Planning for Leisure', in M. A. Smith *et al.*, eds, *Leisure and Society in Britain* (London, Allen Lane, 1973), p. 313.

23 D. Rubenstein and C. Speakman, 'Leisure, Transport and the Countryside' (London, Fabian Research Series, May 1969).

24 L. E. Liddell, 'Planning for Sport', in I. Appleton, ed., *op. cit.*

25 J. Dumazedier, *Sociology of Leisure* (Amsterdam, Elsevier, 1974), p. 141.

26 Patmore, *op. cit.*, p. 153.

27 *Ibid.*, p. 154

28 Dower, *op. cit.*, p. 312.

29 Cosgrove and Jackson, *op. cit.*, p. 144.

30 Dower, *op. cit.*, p. 309.

31 Cosgrove and Jackson, *op. cit.*, p. 148.

32 *Ibid.*, p. 102.

33 Patmore, *op. cit.*, pp. 67–8, 86.

34 Cosgrove and Jackson, *op. cit.*, p. 145.

35 *Ibid.*, p. 136.

36 B. A. Young, 'Community Arts', *Financial Times*, 26 October 1974.

37 Emmett, *op. cit.*, p. 66.

Chapter 11

Conclusion – Leisure and Tomorrow

In this concluding chapter the aim will be to review some of the main points made in the previous chapters, with particular emphasis on what the sociology of leisure has to tell us about current trends in society and the directions of probable future change. Although sociology is not futurology, all branches of sociological enquiry have, at least potentially, something to say about social trends. To seek an understanding of the dynamics of society is to seek to relate the past to the present to the future. With most of the 'established' institutions of society such as work, the family and education there is relatively little emphasis on the future because there is no widespread conviction that these institutions are in their infancy and are about to develop in unprecedented ways. This is not the case with leisure. Part of the reality we are studying is the widely-held belief, whether justified or not, that a 'society of leisure' is coming, if it is not already here.

A society of leisure?

The claim that we already have, or are about to have, a society of leisure rests on a number of propositions and assumptions. One of the most important of these is that leisure is essentially a product of modern industrial society. As we saw in Chapter 2, this view of leisure is to see it as the concomitant of work in industrial society, as the consequence of increased productivity, and as emerging with its own characteristic social institutions. In subsequent chapters we have traced the relationship of leisure to the rest of culture and to other social institutions, and in doing so we have accumulated evidence which will enable us to judge how far it is true that we now have a society of leisure.

Understandably, the advocates of any novel proposition at first overstate their case. Thus in 1970 Kenneth Roberts wrote that 'the information we have at our disposal does suggest that, along with other modern societies, Britain has become a society of leisure in that the activities in which people elect to participate during their free time play a significant part in the development of their sense of self-identity, and leisure thereby is accorded the power to reciprocate the influence that other institutions have upon it'.[1] Though this passage is fairly cautiously worded (and invites the comment 'not really much of a society of leisure, is it?'), it is surpassed in tentativeness by Roberts's 1975 discussion of a *growth* of leisure and by his open question 'Are we verging on a golden age of leisure . . .?'[2] Similarly, Joffre Dumazedier has moved from the view that leisure is emerging as the main institution in contemporary society to an admission that the post-industrial society 'will not be characterised by free time for all. Some of the workers will face working days, weeks, and years as long as in present-day society. . . .'[3]

As noted in Chapter 9, there is no evidence that the amount of time people generally have for daily leisure has been increasing significantly in the post-war period, though the length of holidays *has* been increasing. Although forecasts of vastly increased leisure time were popular a few years ago, not many proponents of a society of leisure today base their claim on a substantial growth of leisure time in the near future. There is rather more evidence that people are increasingly seeking a 'leisure identity' (see Chapter 3), but even here we need to be cautious about projecting a future trend. Leisure is not necessarily a beneficiary of a decline in work values and involvement. Hall and Perry showed that no more than 17 per cent of the urban sample they studied included leisure among the main three aspects of life considered most important in assessing their overall satisfaction or dissatisfaction.[4] Similarly, Alain Touraine remarks that 'in a recent survey, I was struck with the slight importance of leisure activity in the preoccupations of the workers'.[5]

Continuing trends

In recent years there has been a lively controversy about whether the advanced industrial nations of the world should continue to pursue policies of economic growth or whether, for environmental or 'quality of life' reasons, they should aim at zero economic growth.[6] The actual outcome of events will no doubt be a resultant of various social and economic forces, most of which are operating today, but the future strength and success of which it is not easy to predict. Many of the forecasts for materially-based leisure behaviour are the result of extrapolating current trends of economic growth. Thus James Morrell has estimated that in the period to 1985 'the amount of spending power for leisure will probably rise on average by around

4% per annum in constant prices, that is, about 1½ times as fast as spending on necessities'.[7] This assumes that the demand for leisure goods and services is more elastic than that for necessities. Morrell thinks that the extra expenditure will go on such things as second homes, cars and television sets, hobby gadgets and books, outdoor sports equipment, eating out for pleasure, and more frequent and distant holidays abroad.

The supposition of zero economic growth (which, at the time of writing in 1975 seems likely to be the short-term prospect) has different implications for leisure. If the amount of material production were to remain fairly static, improvements in productive efficiency could result in increases of time available for leisure. Since there would be no significantly greater output of leisure goods available for consumption, a growth in leisure services – aiming to give people experiences rather than things – could be expected. These experiences could include personal ones of fantasy, reflection, physical exercise, and so on; social ones of interacting with other people for various purposes unconnected with earning a living (though not necessarily unconnected with work); and environmental ones of enjoying our natural or human-altered surroundings. If zero economic growth is allied to zero population growth leading to an older population than at present, there could be a gradual shift in concern from the problems of youth towards the problems of people approaching or in a state of retirement. There is some indication from official population projections to the end of the century that a gradually ageing population is likely.[8]

Attempts have been made to assess the future pattern of demand for leisure facilities of various kinds (forecasts in connection with sports were mentioned in Chapter 9). The method usually adopted is to find out what the characteristics are of people who are at present above-averagely active in particular leisure pursuits, estimate the probable future population structure in terms of these characteristics, and hence arrive at estimated future participation rates. One such study quoted by Young and Willmott suggests that 'people's leisure in 2001 will probably be more varied and more active, with sports and cultural participation particularly growing in popularity'.[9] This type of demand forecasting does not allow for supply constraints, but it is argued that the leisure industries will generally respond to (or create?) demand, except for those activities like golf and sailing requiring space which may reach an upper limit before demand is fully met.

The ability to measure trends and hence to make reasonably accurate forecasts of the probable type and level of leisure activity depends on the availability of adequate data. In the previous chapter attention was drawn to the very important role of planning in determining the range of leisure opportunities available to people. Sylvia Law is among those who have pointed out the lack of correspondence between the statistics of leisure needed and those currently available.[10] Recreation planners have had to depend almost entirely on statistics collected for other purposes and useful only incidentally for planning purposes. Major aspects of planning such as population, housing, transport, employment, etc. have a large variety of regular government trend statistics available to them. This has not been the case with leisure statistics, but the pressure is beginning to build up for more adequate data to be collected and made available.

Among the cultural influences on leisure referred to in Chapter 2 was the 'time famine' experienced by members of the 'harried leisure class' – the people who are finding that increased industrial output per man hour is not matched by their ability to maintain products and themselves in less time. Will the time famine get worse, spread to more people, or be alleviated? Some commentators see the principle of the more leisurely (in the sense of simpler and less hurried) life making greater appeal as industrial civilisation becomes more stressful and as the delights of ever-increasing material consumption begin to pall. A more popular view (and a more probable one, at least in the short to medium term) is that a consumer society is not likely to be replaced by a leisure society. Also, it is not true that differences between the classes or economic groups in opportunities to spend leisure in various ways have been virtually eliminated. The demand for more leisure *time* is not likely to outstrip the demand by the mass of people for a continued rise in the standard of living.[11]

The all-important question of values

We come finally to the difficult problem of trying to weigh up the prospects for qualitative change in the meaning and experience of leisure. The question of values (conceptions of what is believed to be desirable) has underlain our treatment of leisure throughout this book: in connection with the historical and contemporary cultural context of leisure, in the understanding of leisure as one of several interacting spheres of individual life and of society, and in the alternative plans and policies which are framed to meet leisure needs. There are three sets of value questions which face us when treating our total subject-matter with each of these three emphases: questions concerning the meaning and experience of leisure and the relation of meaning to activity; questions concerning the appropriate role of leisure in the life of the individual and of society; and questions concerning the paradox of planning for freedom in leisure. To these it is necessary to add a fourth category or, rather, a theme pervading each of the other three: questions concerning the nature of the sociology of leisure in the light of answers to the foregoing.

To take up a question first raised in the Introduction: how far is it possible to treat leisure behaviour and institutions objectively, that is, to avoid questions of subjective meaning and of whether some forms of spending leisure are 'better' than others? We can choose to be agnostic about this, to say, with Roberts, that 'push-penny is as good for people as poetry until someone proves otherwise, and the proof has yet to be delivered'.[12] Or we can offer value-judgements for agreement, disagreement or modification by others, presumably with the aim of influencing behaviour or the social regulation of behaviour in desired directions. Ralph Glasser does this, for example, when he writes disparagingly of the advertising campaign for personal fruit machines, and he advocates a spiritually committed society in which 'the guiding aim would be to bring about a replacement of purely time-killing leisure pursuits with ones that put the individual's full personality to constructive use . . .'.[13] Such bodies as the Arts Council and the Sports Council do something similar when they seek financial support, though they seem happier when they can stress the collective rather than the individual good ('preserving our cultural heritage', 'a fitter nation', etc.).

It is worth recalling from Chapter 1 that one category of leisure definitions is overtly normative and that another is a combination of residual (objective) elements plus normative elements. Only residual definitions avoid the question of values by taking leisure to be time that is not devoted to specified non-leisure activities. This type of definition is inadequate because most people do not conceive – or at least do not *consistently* conceive – of leisure in this way. The openly normative definitions of religious writers may frustrate the more hard-headed among us by their use of such indefinable terms as 'fulfilment' and 'spirit', but these can mostly be translated into ethical propositions the popularity of which can be measured (the more difficult question of the *validity* of such ethical propositions is a matter for philosophy rather than sociology). Nevertheless, we are entitled to be sceptical about empirical research on leisure which operates only with residual definitions. Some form of monitoring is necessary to understand leisure behaviour but, as Rolf Meyersohn remarks, 'unless [it] can include the meaning behind choice, the social construction of reality, it remains empty statistical reckoning'.[14]

A second set of value questions concerns the appropriate role of leisure in our lives and in society as a whole. These roles are related to our very basic conceptions of leisure. In our own lives the extremes are something like leisure as minimally tolerated servant of work ends or as the only thing that makes life worth while. In the life of society the parallel extremes are leisure as means of social control or as the highest expression of culture. In between these pairs of extremes there are a wide variety of positions embodying mixed values.

There is also the question of how far, in considering our own lives and the form of society which we regard as desirable, we should think in terms of leisure at all. The rejection of leisure as a useful or even 'relevant' concept can come from a conviction either that the distinction between leisure and work is a false one or that the activities and experiences which some people regard as 'leisure' are reduced rather than enhanced in meaning by being so regarded. Alternatively, the concept of leisure may be retained, but defined in such a way as to reject many values often infused into it and to extend its meaning to other values. Charles Obermeyer does this in his discussion of leisure and human values: 'Leisure is not something added to life, a busy-idle diversion or a long, drawn-out sigh of relief after work, a sigh that is often indistinguishable from boredom. It is the process that builds meaning and purpose into life, and serious talk, solid exchange of ideas, is one of the best ways of doing this.'[15]

A third category of value questions arises from the paradox that, in order to obtain the essence of leisure, freedom, it may be necessary to accept some degree of unfreedom in the form of planning. This issue was touched upon in the previous chapter in connection with the aims of planning. Given that there are constraints of time and environment imposed on all of us, individuals can choose the extent to which they plan their own lives and divide their time and energies to achieve desired goals. Those who are in a position to influence societal goals and the steps taken to achieve these may seek what they regard as a desirable balance between the freedom of the individual and the good of the community. Planning is an important feature of advanced industrial societies and is particularly controversial in the case of leisure because, in comparison with the organisational forms developed for the integration of work effort, there barely exist social forms for the utilisation of leisure.[16]

To plan for freedom of individual choice is to relate leisure to politics in the wide sense of the latter term. There is the domestic side of leisure politics: why the Arts Council gets more public funds than the Sports Council, how to reconcile access to recreation amenities with the need for conservation, and so on. There is also the 'philosophical politics' of the values to be realised in leisure. To do these justice is not possible here, and in any case would not be strictly germane to the sociology of leisure. It is, however, important to underline the relational role of leisure, both in individual lives and in society. The external politics of leisure concern the 'other spheres' which we discussed in Part Two. Some pertinent questions are: How far can and should we seek to realise 'leisure' values in work? In what ways should the family seek to influence the leisure attitudes and behaviour of its young members? Should we 'educate for leisure' and, if so, in what ways? Can religion guide us in the search for satisfying leisure?

By placing leisure in the larger context of life and society, and by raising issues about tomorrow as well as gathering facts about yesterday and today, we stir the sociological imagination. If I have in this book tended to discount the notion of a society *of* leisure, that is partly because I can see greater value in a society *with* leisure.

REFERENCES

1 K. Roberts, *Leisure* (London, Longman, 1970), p. 101.
2 K. Roberts, 'The Society of Leisure: Myth and Reality', in S. R. Parker *et al.*, eds, *Sport and Leisure in Contemporary Society* (London, Polytechnic of Central London, 1975), p. 13.
3 J. Dumazedier, *Sociology of Leisure* (Amsterdam, Elsevier, 1974), p. 21.
4 J. Hall and N. Perry, *Aspects of Leisure in Two Industrial Cities* (SSRC Survey Unit, 1974).
5 A. Touraine, *The Post-industrial Society* (London, Wildwood House, 1974), p. 202.
6 D. Mankin, 'Work and Leisure in a Zero-Growth Society', paper presented at 81st Annual Convention, American Psychological Association, Montreal, 1973.
7 J. G. Morrell, *Business Forecasting for Finance and Industry* (London, Gower Press, 1969).
8 *Social Trends* (London, Central Statistical Office, 1974), p. 74.
9 M. Young and P. Willmott, *The Symmetrical Family* (London, Routledge, 1973), p. 375.
10 S. Law, 'Recreation Statistics for Urban Planning', *Greater London Intelligence Quarterly*, September 1974.
11 R. Aron, *Progress and Disillusion: The Dialectics of Modern Society* (London, Pall Mall Press, 1968), p. 190.
12 Roberts, *op. cit.* (1975), p. 13.
13 R. Glasser, *Leisure – Penalty or Prize?* (London, Macmillan, 1970), pp. 39, 207.
14 R. Meyersohn, 'Leisure', in A. Campbell, ed., *The Human Meaning of Social Change* (New York, Russell Sage, 1972), p. 227.
15 C. Obermeyer, 'Final Observations', in M. Kaplan and P. Bosserman, eds, *Technology, Human Values and Leisure* (Nashville, Abingdon Press, 1971), p. 222.
16 R. S. Weiss and D. Riesman, 'Some Issues in the Future of Leisure', *Social Problems*, Summer 1961, p. 82.

INDEX